D0343279

Six Theories of
JUSTICE

Perspectives
from Philosophical
and Theological
Ethics

Six Theories of
JUSTICE

Karen Lebacqz

AUGSBURG Publishing House • Minneapolis

SIX THEORIES OF JUSTICE
Perspectives from Philosophical and Theological Ethics

Library of Congress Cataloging-in-Publication Data

Lebacqz, Karen, 1945–
  SIX THEORIES OF JUSTICE.

  Bibliography: p.
  Includes index.
  1. Justice.   I. Title.
JC578.L43   1986   320'.01'1   86-26457
ISBN 0-8066-2245-8

Manufactured in the U.S.A.   APH 10-5820

        3   4   5   6   7   8   9   0   1   2   3   4   5   6   7   8   9

To my mother and father,
in whom love and justice
intertwine

Contents

I will make *mishpat** the measure
and ṣ*edaqah*⁺ the plumb line.
(Isa. 28:17)

---

*"Justice," "right."
+ "Righteousness," "justice."

Introduction

There may be no more urgent cry today than that of "justice"—
and no more frequent accusation than that of "injustice." But what is
meant when these terms are used?

Of Elephants and Justice

Alasdair MacIntyre suggests that modern moral utterance must be
understood as a series of "fragmented survivals" from the past: rem-
nants of former ethical systems survive, but without the social cohesion
needed to give them force.[1] Cries of justice and accusations of injustice
appear as such fragments.

Justice is thus a bit like the proverbial elephant examined by blindfolded explorers. Each feels a different part—the foot, the ears, the
tusks—and consequently each describes the beast differently—gnarled
and tough, thin and supple, smooth and hard. The elephant itself—
justice—is not encompassed by any of the individual descriptions. At
times they seem incompatible. And yet, each contributes something to
its definition.

This book is about justice. Six approaches to justice will be our
blindfolded explorers. If MacIntyre's charge is true, then it is to be
expected that these fragments will not be easily reconciled. There will
be no single way of defining justice and no single theory of justice
that satisfies all.

Indeed, the exploration is complicated at the outset because there is precious little agreement as to how the arena of justice is to be characterized and defined.[2] Do we seek for our elephant among mammals or reptiles? The theories to be examined here are roughly in the arena of "distributive justice." But one of our theorists explicitly rejects distributive justice in favor of the more narrow range of "commutative" justice (justice in exchange). And another approach adds to distributive justice a notion of "social justice" with a distinctive flavor.

Thus the views to be examined here are not theories of "distributive justice" in a narrow sense. They are simply theories of justice. Included in their concerns are questions about allocation of goods, powers, and opportunities, about access to decision-making processes, about fundamental respect among people, and about the basic structures of society. They attend to distributive justice in a broad sense: the issue is not simply, Who gets how much of the pie? but also, What kind of pie is it to be? and, Who is to decide?[3]

Six Fragments on Justice

This book explores only six of those "fragmented survivals" of moral systems regarding justice—six ways of "making *mishpat* the measure" (Isa. 28:17). There are many other blindfolded explorers who might have served as well. The choice of six approaches to justice out of all possible contenders is not an easy task, and I make no claim that the six offered here are the only ones worthy of pursuit.

These six were chosen as representatives of different schools of thought. Though three of the fragments are forms of liberalism and three are forms of Christian theology, each offers a distinctive approach to justice. They were chosen also for accessibility: in all cases but one, the reader may supplement this text with a single accompanying document. But, above all, they were chosen in the conviction that each raises fundamental issues for other theories of justice. Each offers a perennial challenge to other contenders.

A Utilitarian Challenge

We begin with a utilitarian challenge. There are few unabashed utilitarians today. Since the theory of utilitarianism was first given definitive shape a century ago, it has been battered and batted around

until it bears the scars of age. Yet, forms of utilitarianism lir.
"cost-benefit analyses" so popular in government circles.
perennial question, *Does* the end justify the means? haunts ...tem-
porary proponents of justice. The significance of utilitarianism is perhaps best attested by the fact that it provides the foil for the other two
contemporary philosophical theories that will be considered in this
volume.

John Stuart Mill's *Utilitarianism* will represent the utilitarian approach to justice here. Mill's exposition lacks the systematic development and meticulous exposition of some later utilitarians, such as
Henry Sidgwick or G. E. Moore; but his approach is more readily
accessible than some others. And it is generally to Mill that contemporary theorists return when they wish to joust with utilitarianism. Thus
Mill's understanding of justice gives us the original challenge and sets
the stage for developing a theory of justice.

A Contract Response

One jouster responding to that challenge is John Rawls. No one
disputes the importance of Rawls' massive effort, *A Theory of Justice*.
This work has dominated philosophical reflections on justice for the
last decade. There simply is no way to talk about justice today without
attending to Rawls' response to the utilitarian challenge. Rawls draws
on a contract model to offer a Kantian alternative to utilitarianism. He
offers a defense of the liberal democratic state that takes "welfare"
needs seriously.

An Entitlement Alternative

But Rawls' view is not the only response to utilitarianism. Robert
Nozick's entitlement view of justice gives voice to the concerns of
many liberals today. Where Rawls' contract theory would permit government involvement to bring about distributive justice, Nozick sets
out to show that there is no moral ground for a distributive justice that
demands structures of government beyond the minimal state. His *Anarchy, State and Utopia* has become—rightly or wrongly—the theory
undergirding contemporary proponents of private enterprise and minimal government. It offers a clear alternative to both the utilitarian
theory and to Rawls.

A Catholic Response

For all their differences, these three philosophical theories operate within a common "liberal" tradition. They share significant assumptions regarding the role and place of the individual as the bearer of moral value and the use of reason as the grounds for any theory of justice. Although Mill argued that utilitarianism was an expression of the golden rule, and many find Rawls' concern for the disadvantaged compatible with Christian sympathies, none of these philosophical theories depends directly on a religious base for its concept of justice. What happens, then, when we turn to the Christian tradition to see what views of justice it offers?

Here we begin with Catholic tradition. In the last hundred years that tradition has developed a multifaceted approach to social justice. Any number of papal encyclicals or other ecclesial documents might have been taken as an example of this approach in its development. The *Pastoral Letter on Catholic Social Teaching and the U.S. Economy* of the National Conference of Catholic Bishops is chosen because of its contemporary interest and its efforts to synthesize and incorporate the long tradition. And it offers a stark contrast to Nozick, arguing for a corporate rather than individualistic understanding of human beings and hence for a broader understanding of social justice.

A Protestant Alternative

Catholic tradition always has its critics from the Protestant side. One who dominated the scene of American Protestantism during much of this century was Reinhold Niebuhr. His stress on sin and his "dialectical" approach to justice and love offers a clear alternative to the Catholic approach.[4] Yet the choice of Niebuhr raises a problem regarding accessibility of accompanying texts. His short volume entitled *An Interpretation of Christian Ethics* gives much of the core of his early theory.[5] Yet Niebuhr later refused to defend this work.[6] Thus, the reader may wish to consult instead *Moral Man and Immoral Society, The Nature and Destiny of Man,* or *Love and Justice: Selections from the Shorter Writings of Reinhold Niebuhr* (ed. D. B. Robertson).

A Liberation Challenge

Finally, a new challenge is being raised today—a challenge to Protestants and Catholics as well as to liberal philosophers. Liberation theology is emerging around the world in places where oppressed peoples are doing their own theological reflection.[7] To represent liberation theology, I have chosen Jose Porfirio Miranda's analysis of justice in *Marx and the Bible*. The stage can be set for his analysis by a brief look at the works of Gustavo Gutierrez, widely acknowledged as a "founder" of liberation theology and one of its most important proponents.

Both Miranda and Gutierrez work out of a Latin American and Catholic context. However, not all liberation theology is Latin American and not all liberation theology is Catholic. It is a diverse and rapidly growing theological approach. Miranda's focus on economic justice accords well with the Latin American context for liberation theology and with our general concerns for distributive justice. In other contexts, however, other questions would loom larger in the liberation perspective.[8]

Thus, Miranda does not speak for all liberation theologians any more than Mill speaks for all utilitarians, Rawls for all contract theorists, Nozick for all Kantians, the National Conference of Catholic Bishops for all Catholics, or Reinhold Niebuhr for all Protestants. Each figure is chosen partly as the representative of a school of thought, but partly also because of the distinctive contribution of that person to the school.

These six fragments are offered in the conviction that each speaks to something so fundamental that, no matter what its defects, it leaves a permanent legacy. Each of these theories has left, or promises to stamp, a lingering mark on our understanding of justice. They may be only fragments, but they are world-shaping fragments.

Of Blindfolded Exploration

All theory is part of an ongoing dialog. Each of these theories has been controversial. Accompanying the exposition of each theory, therefore, is a sampling of critical commentary. No doubt the theorists or supporters from their schools would wish to rebut many of the criticisms reported here. Space precludes a full-fledged debate about each theory, and I have resisted the temptation to offer my own assessments at every point. Even the most recent of the theories presented here will be revised and surpassed by subsequent reflection by the time this book is in print. Readers are encouraged to explore original sources and to judge for themselves the strengths and weaknesses of each approach.

A few preliminary cautions are in order, however. First, of the six approaches represented here, only one author set out explicitly to write a "theory" of justice. The others had other tasks in mind, and whatever "theory" of justice is culled from their work will remain always a bit foreign to their central purposes. The views presented here are perhaps better understood as "windows" on justice rather than as theories per se. A window provides a frame and gives a view. It offers perspective. However, it also requires viewing through a glass and entails the inevitable distortions of that glass.

Indeed, the fragments offered here will reflect the distortions of their social locations. One is from the previous century, one from nearly half a century ago, and the remainder are recent. Most did their work with direct reference to the United States, but two did not. Catholic thought—so often deemed to proceed by papal decree—is represented by a group document. Liberationists, on the other hand, who claim a certain group identity, are nonetheless represented largely by a single thinker. Regrettably, none of our major explorers is a woman.[9] They are a strange group, our blindfolded explorers.

In spite of this fact, I have made no attempt to probe their social locations or personal histories. This is not because I think social location makes no difference to theory. Indeed, it makes all the difference: much of any theory may be attributed to the cultural and personal background of the author. For that very reason, however, the exploration of theory itself will often reveal the author's social location.

Further, theory has a life and an integrity of its own. Thus, the task here is to get "inside" each theory, to the best of our ability, and then to listen to its critics. We have before us six descriptions of an elephant—six proposals for "making *mishpat* the measure." Perhaps we will find that they are not compatible. Perhaps we will find that they are. Can they speak to each other?

With all the interest in justice today, there has been precious little effort to put philosophical and theological theories in dialog. Indeed, theological approaches to justice have not received the systematic exposition and exploration of their philosophical counterparts. This volume is but a small step toward a needed exchange in which the gifts, the assumptions, and the limitations of different views can be explored. Perhaps we shall never define the elephant accurately. But we can at least put the descriptions in juxtaposition. Perhaps as we do so, we will get some sense of the nature of the beast.

One

The Utilitarian Challenge: John Stuart Mill

Classical utilitarianism took root in the latter half of the 19th century and the early part of the 20th. It is associated with such names as Jeremy Bentham, James Mill, John Stuart Mill, Henry Sidgwick, and G. E. Moore. It influenced generations of thinkers, and its legacy is still apparent in "cost-benefit analyses" and defenses of market economies.

Ironically, in spite of its great influence on contemporary thought, utilitarianism is not well defended today. J. J. C. Smart advocates one form of utilitarianism.[1] Richard Brandt argues that another would be the most defensible form, though he does not claim to advocate it himself.[2] Nicholas Rescher proposes what he calls a "chastened" utilitarianism, but his proposal for a principle of justice "distinct from," and "coequal to," utility would place him outside the realm of the classical utilitarians, for whom justice was subordinate to utility.[3]

We turn therefore to the classical approach as defended by John Stuart Mill in *Utilitarianism*. Mill's exposition is of sufficient clarity and persuasiveness to set the stage for the theories of justice that dominate the landscape today.[4]

Utility

The basic idea of utilitarianism is simple: the right thing to do is what produces the most good. Since this is in fact the way many people approach ethical decisions, it is easy to see why the theory has had such appeal. But it deserves more detailed scrutiny.

A summary statement of the utilitarian principle is provided by Mill:

> "Utility" or the "greatest happiness principle" holds that actions are right in proportion as they tend to promote happiness; wrong as they tend to produce the reverse of happiness. By happiness is intended pleasure and the absence of pain. . . .[5]

Into this short statement are packed two crucial assumptions that lay the groundwork for a discussion of justice from a utilitarian perspective.

First, the goal of life is happiness. Both Mill and Jeremy Bentham before him argue this.[6] How do we know this? Bentham offers little "proof" of the assumption that happiness is the goal of life. He rests on the claim that "by the natural constitution of the human frame" we embrace these ends, and he asserts that fundamental principles are not susceptible to direct proof.[7] Mill agrees that "questions of ultimate ends are not amenable to direct proof," but he offers as argument the fact that people universally *do* desire happiness.[8] Thus, the end or goal of human life is taken to be happiness, and we know this because people do desire happiness and because doing so appears to be "natural" to us.

But what is happiness? Bentham defined it in terms of pleasure and the absence of pain. Mill expands on this by arguing explicitly for a recognition of different *kinds* of pleasure and pain. The pleasures of the intellect for Mill are not simply circumstantially more "useful" than those of the flesh, but are intrinsically superior.[9] Hence, a distinction arose among utilitarians between those who consider "happiness" to consist primarily in pleasure and pain and those who add other goals or ends (truth, beauty). The two schools are called "hedonistic" and "ideal" utilitarianism, respectively.[10]

Second, the "rightness" of acts is determined by their contributions to happiness. This makes utilitarianism a form of teleology: the end (*telos*) determines what is right. The "right" is determined by calculating the amount of good to be produced. Thus, the "good" is prior to the "right" and the right is dependent upon it.[11] As Mill puts it, actions are right in proportion as they "tend" to promote happiness.

But this formulation raises a question: must the results of *each action* be calculated to determine its overall "utility" and therefore to decide whether it is right? At first glance this appears to be Bentham's view. In his attempt to render a scientific basis for morality, Bentham offered a method for taking "an exact account" of the tendency of any act:

> Proceed as follows. Begin with any one person of those whose interests seem most immediately to be affected by it: and take an account, 1. Of the value of each distinguishable *pleasure*. . . . 2. Of the value of *pain* . . . . 5. Sum up all the values of all the *pleasures* on the one side, and those of all the *pains* on the other. . . . 6. Take an account of the *number* of persons whose interests appear to be concerned; and repeat the above process with respect to each. . . . Take the *balance* . . . .[12]

Such a description makes it appear that every act must be subjected to a lengthy and time-consuming calculus. In the literature on utilitarianism, this approach of judging the "utility" of each act is called "extreme" or "act-" utilitarianism.[13]

However, Bentham made it clear that he did not expect such a procedure to be "strictly pursued previously to every moral judgment."[14] Mill moves even a step further, proposing that history teaches us the "tendencies of actions" and that these historical lessons give rise to "corollaries from the principle of utility."[15] One does *not*, therefore, "endeavor to test each individual action directly by the first principle" of utility.[16] Rather, the individual act is right if it conforms to a "secondary principle" which has been shown to have utility overall. Taking note of this argument by Mill, Urmson proposes that Mill is best classified as a "restricted" or "rule-" utilitarian.[17] Most commentators have followed Urmson's lead, and the distinction between act- and rule-utilitarianism has become an arena for much debate and discussion.

In sum, the basic idea of utilitarianism is that actions are determined to be right or wrong depending on whether they promote "happiness" or good. This idea has striking implications when we turn to considerations of justice.

Utility and Justice

Traditional notions of justice appear to be flouted by a theory that claims the "right" act is whatever maximizes the good. Individual rights or claims would be overridden by consideration of the "happiness" of others. For example, if the bloodshed of a threatened race riot could be averted by framing and lynching an innocent person, it seems that the utilitarian would have to say it is "right" to do so.[18] So long as the "greater good" required it, all individual rights and claims would be ignored. Because of such apparent implications of utilitarian theory, issues of justice have consistently been a stumbling block for utilitarians.

Both Bentham and Mill recognized this. Indeed, Bentham's overriding concern was to render the penal system more fair and to avoid injustice in the retributive sphere.[19] We focus here on Mill's discussion of the relation between utility and distributive justice.

Mill acknowledges the strength of the feelings people have about justice and the indignation felt at instances of injustice such as undue punishment. This very strength of feeling makes it difficult for people to see justice as a part of utility.[20] Mill therefore sets about to determine whether justice is sui generis or whether it is a part of utility. He concludes that it is not a separate principle arising independently, but is a part of utility: "I dispute the pretensions of any theory which sets up an imaginary standard of justice not grounded on utility."[21] In so doing, Mill follows closely in the footsteps of David Hume, whose defense of the utilitarian basis of justice is worth reviewing.

No one doubts that justice is useful to society, asserts Hume. The question is whether public utility is the *sole* origin of justice.[22] Hume attempts to show that it is by demonstrating that rules of justice do not arise in circumstances where they would not be useful. In situations of extreme deprivation, in circumstances characterized primarily by benevolence, in places where there is such an overabundance that all needs can be met without dispute—in such cases rules of justice would not be "useful" and therefore do not arise. The "use" and "tendency" of the virtue of justice, therefore, are "to procure happiness and security, by preserving order in society."[23] Thus, any rules of justice will depend on the particular state or condition in which people find themselves. All such rules "owe their origin and existence to that *utility,* which results to the public from their strict and regular observance."[24]

Hume does not offer a direct definition of justice. However, from his discussion it can be seen that justice has to do with "separating" and respecting claims about private property.[25] It is where people have conflicting claims over possession in circumstances of moderate scarcity that issues of distributive justice arise. This notion of justice as dealing with *conflicting claims regarding possessions* in *circumstances of scarcity* becomes a pervasive theme throughout modern discussions.

Mill takes over Hume's basic contention that justice does not arise from a "simple, original instinct in the human breast" but arises solely out of its necessity to the support of society.[26] "Justice," he asserts, "is a name for certain moral requirements which, regarded collectively, stand higher in the scale of social utility, and are therefore of more paramount obligation, than any others."[27]

Mill's path to this conclusion has three parts. First, he enumerates instances of "injustice" and searches for a common thread among them. Second, he attempts to discern why there is a particularly strong *feeling* about justice and whether this feeling is grounded in utility. Third, he reviews several controversial cases to show that appeals to "justice" will not resolve the controversy and that only calculations of utility will do so.

Mill finds six common circumstances generally agreed to be "unjust": (1) depriving people of things to which they have a *legal* right; (2) depriving them of things to which they have a *moral* right; (3) people not obtaining what they *deserve*—good to those who do right, and evil to those who do wrong; (4) *breaking faith* with people; (5) being *partial,* i.e., showing favor where favor does not apply; and (6) treating people *unequally.*[28]

These circumstances of injustice seem quite diverse. What is it that unifies them? The notion of legal restraint seems to run through them all, but Mill notes that this notion applies to all of morality: "duty is a thing which may be exacted from a person."[29] What, then, distinguishes justice from other kinds of duty or other aspects of morality?

To answer this question, Mill adopts Kant's distinction between duties of perfect obligation and duties of imperfect obligation. Duties of perfect obligation generate *rights* on the part of the recipient: if I have a duty not to harm you, you have a right not to be harmed by me. Duties of imperfect obligation, on the other hand, do not give rise to corresponding rights: I have a duty to do good, but you have no "right" that I do good for you. Mill suggests that all those duties of perfect obligation that give rise to rights are the arena of justice: "Justice implies something which it is not only right to do, and wrong not to do, but which some individual person can claim from us as his moral right."[30] What distinguishes justice, then, is the notion of rights or claims. Here, Mill echoes Hume, though he does not restrict claims to the arena of property.

Whence, then, comes the special *feeling* that attaches to justice— or that is evoked by instances of injustice? According to Mill, the "sentiment of justice" is "the animal desire to repel or retaliate a hurt or damage" to oneself or to others.[31] In itself, there is nothing moral in this feeling. However, when it is subordinated to "the social sympathies" so that the desire for vengeance becomes a desire that those who infringe rules of justice should be punished, then it becomes a moral feeling. In short, behind justice lies our interest in security, "the most vital of all interests."[32] The rules of justice are therefore supported by the utility of preserving security. When one asks *why* society should defend my rights, the answer lies in the general interest in security. Justice is therefore grounded in utility.

Moreover, Mill suggests that the most intense feelings are raised around certain types of injustice, to wit, "acts of wrongful aggression or wrongful exercise of power over someone" and then acts of "wrongfully withholding from him something which is his due."[33] Such wrongful withholding includes the withholding of good. Thus such common standards of justice as "good for good and evil for evil" are easily encompassed into the utilitarian perspective. And if each is to get what is deserved, then a concept of equal treatment follows: "it necessarily follows that society should treat all equally well who have deserved equally well of *it*. . . . This is the highest abstract standard of social and distributive justice."[34] Strong feelings and commonly accepted standards of justice are therefore explained by the utilitarian view.

Indeed, the utilitarian view will not only explain accepted standards, but will help adjudicate among them. Mill offers three examples of social conflict where the requirements of "justice" are under dispute and generally accepted standards cannot settle the claims. One of these is the question whether remuneration should be based on contribution or on effort. Appealing to "justice" will not solve the issue, for some think justice requires reward for contribution and others think it requires reward for effort. How then do we decide what justice really requires? "From these confusions there is no other mode of extrication than the utilitarian."[35] Justice is ultimately dependent on utility, because conflicts in the common rules of justice can be adjudicated only by reference to utility.

Hence, Mill concludes:

> Justice is a name for certain classes of moral rules which concern the essentials of human well-being more nearly, and are therefore of more absolute obligation, than any other rules for the guidance of life; and the notion which we have found to be of the essence of the idea of justice—that of a right residing in an individual—implies and testifies to this more binding obligation.[36]

Review

In sum, Mill's approach to justice rests on an analysis of the common sense and moral sensitivities of his day. He begins with those things considered unjust in his own society, and he presumes a universal verity for those considerations. His focus is on actions, not on systems or structures per se. His examples are largely at the microlevel; no clear distinctions are made between interpersonal injustices and larger social injustices. He accepts an understanding of justice as dealing with personal claims or rights and attempts to undergird those claims with a utilitarian argument.

Hence, for Mill, there can be no theory of justice separate from the demands of utility. *Justice* is the term given to those rules that protect claims considered essential to the well-being of society—claims to have promises kept, to be treated equally, etc. But those claims are subject to the dictates of a utilitarian calculus; they can be overridden when the "greater good" demands it. Similarly, any conflicts among the rules of justice that protect those claims are also subject to the dictates of a utilitarian calculus and can be overridden. Justice depends on utility and does not contradict utility.

The essential features of justice on the utilitarian scheme are these: It acknowledges the existence of individual *rights* which are to be supported by society.[37] It permits—indeed, for Mill, it requires—*rules* determined to be for the good of society to ensure compliance with certain stringent obligations and to protect individual rights. It can incorporate notions of *equal treatment* and of *desert*. But, most important, justice is not sui generis but is dependent on social *utility* for its foundation. Hence, all rules of justice, including equality, can bow to the demands of utility: "each person maintains that equality is the dictate of justice, except where he thinks that expediency requires inequality."[38] Whatever does the greatest overall good will be "just."

Critique

Since the time of Mill's defense of the relation between utility and justice, utilitarian theory has undergone considerable controversy and revision. We cannot review all that development here. We will confine our critique to those aspects of utilitarianism that raise questions from the perspective of a concern for justice. Does utilitarianism give an adequate account of justice, or does it violate concepts of justice?

The problems for the act-utilitarian are legion. If I am to judge the "right" thing to do in each instance by calculating what will do the most good overall, then there are numerous circumstances in which the "right" act will violate accepted standards of justice. As W. D. Ross pointed out early in this century, and others have later elaborated, act-utilitarianism appears to require that I break a promise or even harm someone any time more "good" could be accomplished by doing so.[39] This, suggests Ross, is absurd. It clearly violates our felt sense of what is right to do: "Do we really think that the production of the slightest balance of good, no matter who will enjoy it, by the breach of a promise frees us from the obligation to keep our promise?"[40]

In a similar vein, John Rawls argues that classical utilitarianism violates the demands of justice by permitting losses to some to be compensated by gains to others. "It may be expedient but it is not just that some should have less in order that others may prosper."[41] Utilitarianism appears not to respect differences between persons.[42]

Others have also argued that utilitarianism ignores the personal character of duty. Ross charges that "if the only duty is to produce the maximum of good, the question who is to have the good—whether it is myself, or my benefactor, or a person to whom I have made a promise—should make no difference."[43] But, of course, it does make a difference.

Indeed, Brandt suggests that the act-utilitarian must face the paradox of having to spend her income on charity rather than on her family if it will do more good. Similarly, if she has promised to pay the child next door $5 for mowing the lawn, she must renege on the promise if she could do more good by giving the $5 to charity. Even accounting for the child's sense of loss, anger, and disillusionment, there are surely circumstances in which the greater good would be done by breaking the promise. Indeed, act-utilitarian theory would appear to go so far as to require that she kill her elderly grandfather if she can prevent his suffering and bring about great good for those who would inherit his estate.[44] As Alan Donagan charges, "act-utilitarianism. . . outrages moral intuition at almost every turn."[45]

Since Mill himself declared that breaking faith or promises is one of the recognized instances of injustice, it is quite clear that he would not have intended utilitarianism to countenance such possibilities. This suggests that rule-utilitarianism may have significant advantages over act-utilitarianism when it comes to justice. For the rule-utilitarian, rules are established on grounds of their overall utility. Then the "rightness" of each act is assessed by seeing whether it concurs with a rule, not by assessing the consequences of the act per se. The rule-utilitarian can permit such secondary rules as "keep promises," or "do not kill," or "provide for your family." Thus, rule-utilitarianism avoids some of the obvious problems that act-utilitarianism encounters in the arena of justice.

Yet rule-utilitarianism is not without its difficulties. First, there is the problem how "rules" are to be understood. Bentham and Mill made no distinctions at all between "act-" and "rule-" utilitarianism; they simply referred to "tendencies" of acts.[46] Mill clearly supported secondary rules to be derived from the great principle of utility. Yet it is not clear just what *sort* of rules he had in mind, nor what sort are most defensible. Some think that his "rules" were merely "rules of thumb"—generalizations from experience that would be helpful in the circumstances but could be overridden at any time by the direct application of the primary principle of utility. Thus, "keep promises" would be a helpful rule of thumb, but would not necessarily tell us whether to keep a specific promise. A rule-utilitarianism based on rules of thumb easily collapses into act-utilitarianism, since rules are always subject to being overridden by the immediate application of the principle of utility.

However, as John Rawls points out in a celebrated essay, "Two Concepts of Rules," this is only one way to understand how rules might function in a utilitarian approach.[47] Not all rules are "summary rules" that can be reconsidered in the moment. Some rules are "practice" rules: they define a practice, such that the practice does not exist apart from its rules. Games such as baseball are of this sort—the game does not exist apart from the rules that define it. Rawls argues that promising is a "practice." Rules about promising, therefore, are not liable to be set aside at any moment, "for unless there were already the understanding that one keeps one's promises as part of the practice itself, there couldn't have been any cases of promising."[48] That is, promises could not exist apart from the rules that say they are to be kept; that is part of the meaning of a promise.[49]

Now, if utilitarian rules are of this "practice" sort, then they will not be liable to being overridden in the instance. At first glance, this would appear to get rule-utilitarianism out of the dilemmas of act-utilitarianism. However, the attempt is not altogether successful. As Lyons notes, the practice must be justified by its utility. But suppose there is an instance within the practice where more utility would seem to be achieved by breaking the rules of the practice (e.g., by breaking a promise). Lyons suggests that each such case implies that there is a "subclass" within the practice that ought to be permitted as an exception to it. In short, the practice itself may not yield as much utility as would a different definition of the practice that permitted certain exceptions. But then this means that the practice cannot be justified on grounds of utility, since in fact it does not yield as much utility as another, similar "practice" would. Hence, every exception to the practice threatens to undermine the utilitarian justification for the practice itself.[50]

Further, there is always the possibility that secondary principles, even "practice" rules, can conflict with each other. What is one to do then? For example, in the arena of distributive justice rewarding people for *effort* will tend toward greater utility by providing incentives. Yet rewarding for *contribution* will avert resentment and thus encourage industry. It is entirely possible, then, that a rule-utilitarian system will produce two subsidiary rules, one rewarding for effort and the other for contribution. What is the rule-utilitarian to do when these conflict?

In such a circumstance, either there must be additional priority rules for determining what to do in cases of conflicts among rules, or the rule-utilitarian falls back upon an act-utilitarian escape: do whatever will produce the most good in *this* circumstance. In the first instance, rule-utilitarianism becomes absurdly burdened with subsidiary rules and becomes ultimately impossible to learn and hence to follow.[51] This suggests that the obvious secondary rule is the utilitarian principle itself: when rules conflict, do whatever would produce the most good in the circumstances. This appears to be the solution Mill proposed in his case about conflicting rules of justice in remuneration. But then even "practice" rule-utilitarianism seems ultimately to collapse into act-utilitarianism.[52] It may be for that reason that McCloskey calls rule-utilitarianism a "half-hearted" utilitarianism.[53]

Moreover, critics charge that some rules good for society would require acts generally not considered to be obligatory or required by justice. For instance, it might serve utility to have a rule that all members of society should put aside a small portion of their income to support those who have no desire to work for their living.[54] Yet, generally, such acts would be considered acts of "beneficence" rather than of "justice"; they would fit Kant's category (adopted by Mill) of "imperfect" rather than "perfect" obligation. How does utilitarianism propose to draw the line between justice and beneficence, obligation and supererogation?[55]

Perhaps even more fundamental than these criticisms are the possible conflicts within the utilitarian formula itself. Mill was quite clear that the utilitarian standard was not the agent's own happiness but "the greatest amount of happiness altogether."[56] The calculator of happiness is to be "strictly impartial" between his own happiness and that of others.[57] Indeed, the principle of utility "is a mere form of words without rational signification unless one person's happiness. . .is counted for exactly as much as another's."[58]

But this then gives rise to a problem: is it the greatest *good* that is to be done, or the greatest good *for the greatest number?* Classical utilitarians have used both formulae, seemingly without regard to the possible conflicts between them. But conflicts there are, as Nicholas Rescher pointedly shows. Take the following two distribution schemes:

Scheme I	Scheme II
A receives 8 units	A receives 4 units
B 1	B 4
C 1	C 1

Scheme I does the "greatest good" overall, but Scheme II does the "greatest good for the greatest number." Which is required by the utilitarian formula? Are we to honor the greater number, or the overall maximum utility?[59]

The problem is seen in sharp relief when we consider the possibility that we might increase *overall* utility or happiness simply by increasing the number of people on earth. Yet the *average* happiness of each might be lowered considerably as the population rose.[60] For instance, a society consisting of 10 people with 2 units of happiness each has a total utility of 20 units, whereas a society consisting of 40 people with 1 unit of happiness each has a total utility of 40 units. Does the utilitarian formula require that we add to the population so as to increase overall utility even at the cost of average happiness?[61]

Clearly, this is not what is intended, and some have proposed that the maximum overall utility should be interpreted precisely in terms of *average* utility. To do so appears to avoid some problems encountered by the classical utilitarian formula.[62]

But average utility has its problems While it seems to work well in the example above, consider the following example:

Scheme I		Scheme II	
A receives 6 units		A receives 5 units	
B	6	B	5
C	6	C	5
D	1	D	4
E	1	E	1

Our intuitive sense is that Scheme II is more just. But taking average utility gives no way to choose between them, since the average utility in each case is 4 units.

With yet another slight modification, average utility can be shown to be counterintuitive:

Scheme I		Scheme II	
A receives 6 units		A receives 4 units	
B	6	B	4
C	6	C	4
D	1	D	3
E	1	E	3

Again, Scheme II seems the more fair. Yet it yields an average utility of only 3.6 units compared to an average utility of 4 units in Scheme

I. Modifying utilitarianism to focus on average utility does not seem to solve the problem of violations of our intuitive sense of justice. Concern for the average happiness does not solve the problem of gaps between those at the top and those at the bottom.

Both classical and average utility therefore appear to leave open the possibility that some will be sacrificed for the sake of others. The possibility that some might be deprived in order that others might experience great happiness "offends our sense of justice," declares Rescher.[63] Hence, he proposes that we need some sort of "utility floor" to ensure that none are pushed below the point of survival or minimal utility in order that others may gain.

But even when all are at or above a utility floor, the utilitarian formula appears to countenance serious inequities. Take, for example, the following two schemes, where 1 unit is the utility floor:

Scheme I		Scheme II	
A receives 2 units		A receives 1 unit	
B	2	B	1
C	3	C	6
D	3	D	6
E	3	E	6

From the perspective both of overall utility and of the "greatest good for the greatest number," Scheme II is clearly superior. Yet unless we have some reason to think that C, D, and E *ought* to get such disproportionately large shares, our instincts tell us that Scheme I is more just.[64] Whether given as "the greatest good" or as "the greatest good for the greatest number," therefore, utilitarianism appears to provide no guarantees against grossly inequitable distributions.

This takes us to what Rescher calls the "decisive and fatal" objection to the principle of utility, taken alone, as a standard for justice.[65] In the paragraph above, we raised the question whether there might be some reason to think that persons C, D, and E "ought" to receive more than persons A and B. This notion of "ought" or "desert" is fundamental to justice and appears to be ignored by the utilitarian approach.

If all the potential recipients of a distribution scheme are equally deserving, then the utilitarian approach of counting up their happinesses and unhappinesses and maximizing the total good may be the most fair way to deal with the situation. But, as Rescher argues, "human actions. . . are inherently claim-modifying; they. . .engender merit and demerit."[66] Real people in a real world act; and as they act, they create claims (merit or demerit) for themselves—or possibly claims on the part of others (e.g., by making a promise). To ignore such claims is to deny justice in a very fundamental sense.

Indeed, to maximize happiness for five bad people while three good people go unhappy seems to some the very antithesis of justice. As Ross puts it,

> Suppose that A is a very good and B a very bad man, should I then. . . think it self-evidently right to produce 1001 units of good for B rather than 1000 for A? Surely not. I should be sensible of a *prima facie* duty of justice, i.e., of producing a distribution of goods in proportion to merit, which is not outweighed by such a slight disparity in the total goods to be produced.[67]

One need not accept the thesis that justice means distribution *solely* in terms of virtue in order to give virtue and vice some "claim" in the distribution process. Since the time of Aristotle, philosophers have generally acceded that justice requires, at least to some extent, distribution in accord with virtue or moral excellence. Maximization of happiness does not always seem good in itself.[68]

Thus Rescher argues the strong thesis that "distributive justice consists in the treatment of people *according to their legitimate claims*" and concludes that "a doctrine of distribution that is not predicated upon a judicious accommodation of claims is not a theory of distributive justice."[69]

Critics of utilitarianism do not agree on the range of legitimate claims.[70] Rescher finds seven such claims that have held an honored place in history. One of these is indeed the utilitarian standard of distributing in accord with what is in the public interest or for the common good. However, there are six additional claims—need, contribution, effort, ability, the market values of supply and demand, and equality.[71] Our purpose here is not to explore or defend all of these claims, but merely to suggest that if justice can be shown to require attention to any one of them outside the utilitarian canon, and if utilitarianism can be shown not to account adequately for that one, then utility alone does not suffice to give justice.

Mill would have responded to such a charge that utilitarianism is here misunderstood. As noted above, the principle of utility permits secondary principles—indeed, for Mill it requires them. Among these will be such principles as "evil for evil" and "good for good." Thus, notions of desert appear to be handled by a rule-utilitarian scheme. Mill can simply argue that distributions ignoring claims would frustrate normal expectations and therefore undermine society.[72] In short, what is unjust cannot be truly useful or happiness-maximizing, though it may appear so at first glance.

Putting aside the general objections to rule-utilitarianism noted above, does such a rule-utilitarian approach solve the difficulty? Following Rescher and other critics, I think not. First, one cannot show that a recognition of claims would *always* be required as a component of utility. The rule-utilitarian must be willing to permit the possibility that a utilitarian system of rules would *not* incorporate some of the claims enumerated above. Second, to say that such claims arise because they are useful and then to say that utility requires that they be part of justice is circular reasoning. If there is no standard of justice independent of utility, why should such "normal expectations" arise in the first place?[73]

Then there is the difficult issue of how the "utility" of frustrating such normal expectations is to be judged. Indeed, a problem common to both act- and rule-utilitarianism is how the *value* of different goods and evils is to be assessed.[74] Utilitarianism requires not only predictions of the future, which are notoriously inaccurate, but also some way to measure different values against each other. "The point of the concept of *utility* is to quantify diverse sorts of personal happiness."[75]

But some goods seem incommensurable to others. How does one weigh the harm of the disappointment experienced by the child to whom a promise is broken against the good done by giving food for subsistence to a poor family? Utilitarians often *assert* that the principle of utility would not permit some of the most egregious behavior (such as punishing an innocent person), but rarely do they offer any means of *demonstrating* the truth of such assertions. They are largely dependent on the "common sense" of their day.

This means that they do not recognize the cultural limitations of the value judgments incorporated into utilitarian assertions. For example, Sidgwick argues *against* the notion that the rich should distribute their superfluous wealth among the poor, on grounds that "the happiness of all is on the whole most promoted by maintaining, in adults generally (except married women), the expectation that each will be thrown on his own resources for the supply of his own wants."[76] In an ethical system where the right depends on calculations of the good, those calculations are always subject to cultural limitations.

Finally, the utilitarian approach, which focuses so exclusively on the *results* of distribution, appears to neglect another important aspect of justice: the *procedures* for distribution.[77] To be sure, a rule-utilitarian is likely to accept "equal opportunity" or "openness of positions" or some other procedural safeguards as part of the subsidiary rules of justice justified by the principle of utility.[78] However, as noted above, such equalities are always vulnerable to the greater utility of inequality of access or opportunity: "All persons are deemed to have a *right* to equality of treatment, except when some recognized social expediency requires the reverse."[79]

Assessment

In spite of all these criticisms and objections, "the utilitarian theory of distribution is impressive."[80] As Brandt notes, the kinds of things that emerge as relevant in a utilitarian approach really *are* relevant to issues of justice. So it would not be fair to leave the utilitarians without indicating some of the strengths of utilitarian concerns.[81]

Those strengths appear to lie precisely at the point where a narrow calculus of justice in terms of what is "due" to persons will actually limit rather than enhance their life chances. Many authors distinguish between a "narrow" and a "wider" sense of justice (or between "justice" and "fairness" or some other cognate terms). Justice in the narrow sense deals with claims, merit, and distribution in accord with what is "due" to persons. It focuses almost exclusively on the allocation aspect of distributive justice: who is to receive what.

But a theory of distributive justice that focuses exclusively on the *allocation* of goods and neglects the link between *production* and allocation makes a serious mistake. Consider, for example, the following two schemes:

Scheme I	Scheme II
A receives 3 units	A receives 5 units
B 3	B 5
C 3	C 6

Assuming the parties have equal claims, from the perspective of distributive justice, narrowly conceived, the first scheme is more just. All parties have received equally, in accord with their claims.

But surely they might prefer the second scheme, in which goods are not distributed equally, but everyone receives a larger share. If an unequal distribution of goods (e.g., through special incentives) creates more good for all, then it seems at least "better," if not more "just," in the narrow sense. What is available to be distributed can be affected by the pattern of distribution itself: by permitting some to have more than others even when their claims may be equal, incentives can be created so that more goods are produced and the life chances of all are enhanced.

This is precisely the strength of classical utilitarianism, which saw that "justice" in a narrow sense of the exact honoring of claims might be sacrificed for "utility" in the sense of greater happiness for all. As Rescher puts it, "justice in its fullest expression requires that account be taken also of the common good."[82] What seems "unfair" in a narrow sense may still be "just" in the wider sense.[83] Thus, even such a staunch defender of claims as Rescher finds some justification for allocations of goods based not on claims but on social utility.

Indeed, several authors conclude that "justice" in its broadest sense requires attention both to "fairness" in the more narrow sense and to utility. Brandt notes that systems that distribute income most equally generally do not provide the most incentive for production and hence the most chance for increasing the goods available to all. He therefore concludes that both equality and utility appear to be required for justice.[84] Rescher also attributes to utility a place in a larger understanding of justice: "Our thesis is that justice (in the narrow sense) and the general good of utilitarianism must be *coordinated* with one another, and that just this constitutes Justice in its wider sense."[85]

While classical utilitarianism may not always provide for our best understanding of justice in the more narrow sense, it adds an important dimension for any full theory of justice. It therefore raises a serious challenge and sets an important agenda for all who would attempt a theory of justice. It is precisely that agenda that is addressed by contemporary theorist John Rawls.

Two

A Contract Response: John Rawls

Whatever its shortcomings, classical utilitarianism sets an important agenda for other theories of justice. The strengths of utilitarianism in the arena of justice are two: (1) it provides—in theory at least—a concrete method for making difficult decisions; and (2) it recognizes the importance of happiness or the general good as part of a theory of justice. Yet we also saw that utilitarianism presents problems for justice: it appears not to honor individual persons, and it has implications that are often "counterintuitive, sometimes manifestly abhorrent."[1]

The task that John Rawls sets himself in *A Theory of Justice* is to propose an alternative theory of justice that avoids the weaknesses of utilitarianism while demonstrating similar strengths.[2] He hopes to construct a theory that takes persons seriously and does not risk their well-being or rights for the sake of others' good, but which also offers a concrete method for making the most fundamental decisions about distributive justice. The result is "justice as fairness."

Method

"Justice as fairness" has its roots in two places: the social contract theories of Locke and Rousseau, and the deontology of Kant. The basic idea is astonishingly simple, though its working out in theory is very complex. Rawls' aim is to use the concept of a social contract to give a procedural interpretation to Kant's notion of autonomous choice as the basis for ethical principles. Principles for justice (and moral philosophy in general) are to be the outcome of rational choice.[3]

In essence, the approach is this: imagine a group of people who are going to choose principles for assessing the justice of basic structures of society. Clearly, if the principles are to be just, they must be chosen in a situation that is itself fair. That is, no one must be allowed to dominate the choice, nor to use to unfair advantage such contingencies as natural endowments or social position.[4] Hence, principles of justice will be the result of fair choice—"justice as fairness."[5]

How, then, do we make the circumstances of choice—the "original position" from which the parties choose—fair? Rawls proposes that the representative persons in the original position choose from behind a "veil of ignorance."[6] The veil of ignorance and other stipulations of the original position become the lynchpins of the system: "the idea of the initial situation is central to the whole theory and other basic notions are defined in terms of it."[7]

The veil of ignorance means that the parties choosing principles lack certain kinds of knowledge that might make the bargaining process unfair.[8] They do not know what position they hold in society, nor what their own particular goals or life-plans might be. They do not know what society they belong to, nor what generation they are. Such particular kinds of knowledge always make it possible for persons to skew principles in their own favor. This would clearly not be fair, and so there must be an adequate veil of ignorance to remove such possibilities.

What the parties do know are two things. First, their society will be subject to the "circumstances of justice."[9] This means that it is characterized by conflict as well as by cooperation, but that cooperation is possible and beneficial.[10] Along lines suggested earlier by Hume, Rawls proposes that circumstances of justice obtain "whenever mutually disinterested persons put forward conflicting claims to the division of social advantages under conditions of moderate scarcity."[11] Questions of justice arise in situations of scarcity and conflict of interest.

Second, they must know something about economic theory, something about social organization, and something about human psychology.[12] In short, they must know enough about human society to be able to make some predictions about the likelihood that principles chosen can be strictly adhered to without undue stress or "strains of commitment."[13]

Moreover, the parties are mutually disinterested.[14] That is, they take no *particular* interest in each other's aims and purposes, whatever those might be. They are also rational, knowing that they want more of the primary goods of life if possible.[15] And they are not "envious"—that is, they prefer to gain in primary goods even if others gain more than they do.[16]

In short, we have a circumstance in which people do not know their specific life plans, but know only that they are likely to want more of those basic goods that help to support any life plan. They enter the bargain with a view to furthering their own interests in obtaining such goods, but without the kind of envy that would make them refuse gain for themselves accompanied by greater gain for others. They are ignorant of the kinds of things that would give them an unfair advantage in any bargaining position. Under these stipulations, the hypothetical "contract" can proceed.

They are then offered a choice of a range of principles for the distribution of rights and duties and of the benefits and burdens of social cooperation. These principles will govern the basic structure of society—the network of institutions that determines to a large extent what their life chances will be. It should be noted here that they also choose for a "well-ordered society," that is, for a society in which they can expect that the concept of justice chosen is public and that people comply strictly with its requirements.[17] Which principles will they choose?

Principles of Justice

Rawls argues that under such conditions, the parties choosing in the original position would choose two principles of justice. First, they would be concerned to secure their equal liberty, and they would establish a principle to that effect:

> Each person is to have an equal right to the most extensive total system of equal basic liberties compatible with a similar system of liberty for all.[18]

That is, they would separate out basic human liberties and secure them against any unequal division.

Indeed, Rawls argues that except under very stringent circumstances, the parties in the original position would never want to permit any compromising of basic liberties for the sake of other social or economic benefits. Thus, not only is equal liberty the first principle, but it stands in serial ("lexical") order, so that liberty can be restricted only for the sake of liberty and not for the sake of economic or other social gains.[19]

Next comes the question whether they would permit any inequalities in income, wealth, power, and so on. Here, it might seem as though the obvious answer is no. That is, people choosing principles from an initial situation of equal ignorance and not knowing what their position in society will be might choose to ensure that goods are always divided equally.[20] Indeed, if society were a "zero sum game" in which the size of the store of goods to be distributed could never be increased, this is precisely what Rawls says they would do.[21]

However, human society is not a "zero sum game." Through the efforts of social cooperation it is possible to increase the quantity of goods to be distributed. For example, suppose there is a shoe factory with five workers, each currently earning $10,000 per year.[22] One of these workers has a particularly arduous task, and it is because of the time required for that task that a bottleneck occurs and production is held at current levels. Now it might be possible to induce this person to work faster by paying $13,000 per year (or to attract to the job a more skilled person than could be attracted by $10,000). If the increased productivity releases the bottleneck overall, so that the net income of the company is now $60,000, then there is a "utility surplus" of $7000 (net income less salaries). This surplus could be divided among the other workers, bringing their salaries up to $11,750. Incomes are no longer equal, but everyone is better off.

Given that human society works this way and that the parties in the original position would know such general facts about society, surely they would choose the unequal incomes represented by the increased salaries here.[23] This was, of course, precisely the challenge raised by utilitarianism: justice in its full sense seems to require some accounting for the *amount* of good as well as for its allocation.

However, utilitarianism might stipulate that justice is done even if one person loses in the transition, so long as "the greater good for the greater number" or the "greater net good" was done. Suppose the rearrangement of the shoe factory will put one person's salary at $9000 while others move to $12,333 and one moves to $13,000. Under the utilitarian scheme, this represents the greater net good and the greater good for the greater number. But one person is worse off.

Why would persons in the original position choose a principle that might make them *worse* off than they were before? Rawls argues that the parties in the original position would not choose the utilitarian principle.[24] Since they are concerned to protect their own interests, they would not risk lesser income only for the benefit of others. Rather, they would choose a principle such as the following:

> Social and economic inequalities, for example inequalities of wealth and authority, are just only if they result in compensating benefits for everyone, and in particular for the least advantaged members of society.[25]

Called the "difference principle," this principle becomes the core of Rawls' substantive theory of justice. It permits some inequalities in distribution, but only those that protect or improve the position of the least advantaged in society.

Choice of the difference principle over a principle such as maximizing average utility rests on one of the more controversial aspects of Rawls' theory: his adoption of the strategy of "maximin." In brief, this strategy stipulates that the parties in the original position would choose in such a way as to "maximize the minimum."[26]

The choice of "maximin" as a strategy can be understood this way: Suppose I am in this original bargain. I do not know who I will be in society, nor what kind of a society I may encounter when the veil of ignorance is lifted. With no way of calculating my chances of being the least advantaged, it is reasonable for me to act protectively to preserve the position of the least advantaged member of society, since that person might be me. Thus, I will permit inequalities only if they work to the benefit of the least advantaged. Hence, I will try to avoid the worst results and "maximize the minimum." Thus, I am concerned not merely that any inequalities result in compensating benefits for everyone, but especially that they result in benefits for the "least advantaged." The strategy of maximin is thus "the vital bridge linking the rules of justice with the conditions described by the original position."[27]

Moreover, those in the original position would want to be sure that any inequalities of position and power are not locked in for all time, but are subject to fair competition and open to all persons to try for them. Though they would be willing to permit social inequalities that work to their advantage, they will stipulate that such inequalities be attached to positions open to all on a liberal principle of "fair equality of opportunity."[28] Finally, since they are not sure to which generation they belong, they will require that one generation not squander resources but enact a "just savings principle" toward the good of future generations.

Thus, the final formulation of Rawls' second principle of justice for institutions is as follows:

> Social and economic inequalities are to be arranged so that they are both:
>   (a) to the greatest benefit of the least advantaged, consistent with the just savings principle, and
>   (b) attached to offices and positions open to all under conditions of fair equality of opportunity.[29]

Added to the principle of equal liberty, we now have the two principles that form the core of Rawls' theory of justice for the basic structures of society.

These two principles are a "special case" of a general concept of justice. The general concept is that social values "are to be distributed equally unless an unequal distribution of any, or all, of these values is to everyone's advantage."[30] In contrast to the utilitarian "greatest good" criterion, Rawls' conception requires that *each person* benefit from any social inequalities.[31] The requirement that *each* person benefit becomes the requirement that the *least advantaged* benefit under the stipulations of maximin in the original position.

The full theory, therefore, takes the form of a fundamental affirmation of liberty and a limited acceptance of certain inequalities, judged from the perspective of their impact on the position of the least advantaged.[32] These principles are those that would be chosen by autonomous individuals situated in a "fair" setting. They are thus, in Rawls' view, "categorical imperatives" expressing the autonomy of "free and equal rational beings."[33] Most importantly, perhaps, the principles that would be chosen are *not* those of classical utilitarianism or its numerous revisions.

Justification

If Rawls is right, then the two principles cited above are the principles that would be chosen by those in the original position as principles for distributing rights and duties, burdens and benefits. But are these principles *just*? Does the fact that they are chosen mean that they are right? To ask this question is to ask about the justification for the principles.

The answer to the question may be given in several ways. First, "justice as fairness" yields "pure procedural justice." In pure procedural justice there is no standard for deciding what is "just" apart from the procedure itself.[34] "Justice" applies not to the outcome, but to the system.[35] Rawls develops this concept in discussing the place of "equal opportunity" as a principle of justice. However, it may also apply to "justice as fairness" as a theory: whatever is chosen by the parties in the original position is just simply by virtue of being the outcome of the decision procedure. Thus, if the parties do in fact choose Rawls' two principles, then these are the principles that provide justice.

Much depends, therefore, on the original position and the strictures established around the choice procedure. Here Rawls proposes two constraints to assess the fairness of the procedure. The first is that the premises introduced into the original position should be as "weak" as possible and should be widely accepted.[36] Only those things that are generally agreed to constitute "fair" or "minimal" assumptions should be necessary in the original position. Hence, for example, we cannot propose that everyone share a particular goal or life plan, for this would require some strong assumptions about the human good; however, we can propose that each party will have his or her own life plan, and will seek certain primary goods as means necessary to that life plan. Thus, "the conditions embodied in the description of the original position are ones that we do in fact accept."[37]

The second constraint or qualification is a method of assessment called "reflective equilibrium."[38] This method involves testing the description of the original position by seeing whether it yields principles that really do match our considered convictions about justice. Do the principles that arise seem to us to require what is fair when we deliberate about it? If not, then we can either change our considered convictions (pruning or stretching them as the principles might require) or we can alter the stipulations about the original position until it yields new principles that give us a better match. With this "back and forth" method of testing, "eventually we shall find a description of the initial situation that both expresses reasonable conditions and yields principles which match our considered judgments duly pruned and adjusted."[39]

The second and third parts of *A Theory of Justice* are devoted largely to testing out the implications of the principles: do they yield social institutions that match our considered convictions about justice?[40] Do they offer a vision of a well-ordered and fair society? Rawls argues that the principles, worked out in social institutions, would help us to discard those ordinary precepts of justice that are not helpful on a fundamental level, and would confirm other common suppositions about justice. Perhaps most important here is his rejection of any concept of distribution in accord with virtue; all legitimate expectations are shown to be based on social institutions, not on such factors as the contingencies of birth or advantages of upbringing.[41]

The final test of the theory depends on the coherence of all these elements together: the original position, the arguments for the principles chosen, the kinds of institutional arrangements which they might engender, and the fit between these arrangements and our considered convictions of justice.

Review

"Justice as fairness" provides a clear contrast to the utilitarian view. Principles of justice are derived not by assessing the utility of actions (or of tendencies of actions) but by rational choice in a fair setting. Those principles are geared toward the basic structure of society, not toward every act or every level where justice is a concern. Rawls deals on the macrolevel rather than the microlevel. *A Theory of Justice* offers a complex and subtle theory, based on a striking insight about the potential for using the social contract as a basis for a theory of justice.

Most important, where Mill's utilitarian approach leaves the individual vulnerable to the demands of the greater good of others, Rawls' principles clearly protect those who are least advantaged. No "trade-offs" are allowed between their liberty or well-being and the well-being of others. Basic liberties must be distributed equally and cannot be sacrificed for the sake of economic gain. While income and social status, power and privilege, may be distributed unequally, such unequal distribution is allowed only where it renders the least advantaged better off than they would otherwise be.

Critique

Does the theory succeed? The voluminous criticism that has arisen in scarcely more than a decade testifies to the importance of Rawls' theory.[42] It also suggests that there may be serious flaws in "justice as fairness." A sampling of the critical commentary directed toward Rawls' method, principles, and justification will illumine problem areas and also demonstrate the divergence among critics.

Method

Rawls' contract method has been criticized from a number of angles. Some of these will be dealt with below in the discussion of justification. Several others deserve separate attention.

"Justice as fairness" is meant to set up a situation in which principles for justice are the outcome of rational choice. The "original position" with its "veil of ignorance" is to remove those particularities that would bias choices. Hence, the principles chosen need not presume particular concepts of the good, but presume only a minimum about human nature, namely, that people are free, equal, and rational. Does the original position succeed in providing the kind of "neutrality" desired?

Several critics argue that it does not. Marxist critics charge that Rawls' basic definition of human nature and of human society has built into it some deep biases about nature and society.[43] Fisk asserts that the concept of humans as free, equal, and rational is not a neutral concept.[44] In Marxist perspective, human nature cannot be defined entirely apart from social class. Nor is a "well-ordered" society necessarily the goal in terms of which justice is to be defined, given Marxist assumptions about class struggle. Thus, Rawls' attempt to take an ahistorical, "world" perspective is antithetical to some basic Marxist assumptions.

A related critique challenges Rawls' implicit epistemology. The veil of ignorance is intended to remove particular knowledge, but the parties in the original position are still presumed to have general knowledge about such areas as politics and economic theory. Is this possible? Wolff charges that there can be no such "general" knowledge that is not itself based on particular knowledge.[45] What "theories" about economics would be known? Any such theories have biases already built into them. Thus, it is not possible for the parties in the original position to have unbiased general knowledge; all general knowledge is based on and reveals particularities and biases.

Sandel maintains that Rawls' theory depends on an unsubstantiated notion of the choosing self. Rawls attempts to adapt Kant's autonomous self. The principles are to reflect the choice of this self, and to be "categorical imperatives" expressing the nature of persons as free, equal, and rational. But there must be no overriding ends that direct the choices made. Hence, the "selves" who do the choosing must always stand at a certain distance from their ends and goals: they "have" goals, but they are not defined by them. Ultimately, this means that the self becomes "invulnerable"—it is not changed by its experiences, nor by its cooperation with others. This is a very limited view of the self, charges Sandel, and does not account for some important aspects of community and of self-knowledge. "If utilitarianism fails to take seriously our distinctness, justice as fairness fails to take seriously our commonality." [46]

Several critics note that under the circumstances of the veil of ignorance, the "contract" really becomes a kind of individual rationality "writ large." [47] Since the veil of ignorance removes the distinguishing features of the parties to the point where their decision would be unanimous, there is a sense in which they can be collapsed into one person. Rawls himself recognizes this. He proposes that the "contract" is really a "perspective" that can be adopted by anyone willing to put herself or himself under the requisite veil of ignorance. [48]

However, one of Rawls' criticisms of utilitarianism is that it uses an "ideal observer" approach that derives social principles as though they were equivalent to the choices made by a single person. "There is no reason," says Rawls, "to suppose that the principles which should regulate an association of [people] is [sic] simply an extension of the principle of choice for one [person]." [49] Yet this is precisely what happens once the "contract" is collapsed into the perspective of a single person.

Finally, critics charge that Rawls' theory is essentially circular. The argument depends on the particular circumstances chosen for the original position. These are manipulated to yield the two principles, since Rawls himself acknowledges that a slight variation would yield a form of utilitarian principle. As Fishkin puts it, "adoption of one particular procedure can always be challenged on the ground that it is biased toward X's convictions rather than Y's." [50]

Principles

This leads us to the question whether Rawls' method would indeed yield his principles. Rawls' two principles and their lexical ordering have also come under close scrutiny and are found wanting by many critics.[51]

The Principle of Equal Liberty

Hart raises several criticisms regarding Rawls' principle of equal liberty. As posed, and with the lexical order in effect, this principle permits restrictions on liberty only for the sake of a more *extensive* system of liberties. But liberties can conflict. When they do, appeal to the *extent* of the system of liberty may not resolve the conflict. Rather, what is needed is judgments about the relative *value* of the two liberties at stake.[52] Since reasonable people may differ as to these liberties, appealing to the judgment of a rational person in the original position does not solve the problem.

Moreover, our "considered convictions" about justice include many instances in which liberty must be curtailed in order to avoid harm to others, e.g., in legislation regarding pollution. It would be "extraordinary," says Hart, if Rawls meant to exclude such instances from permissible restrictions on liberty.[53]

Finally, Hart notes that every liberty is a two-edged sword: I receive benefits from exercising a liberty myself, but must also bear the burdens of others exercising it. The choice of a principle of liberty depends upon a judgment that the benefits from having the liberty will outweigh the harm of having others exercise the same liberty.[54] Would those in the original position then choose Rawls' principle regarding liberty? "It does not follow that a liberty which can only be obtained by an individual at the price of its general distribution through society is one that a rational person would still want."[55]

The Lexical Ordering

Other criticisms are directed not at the first principle per se, but at its relation to the second principle.

First, some challenge the presumed independence of the two principles. Rawls appears to presume that inequalities in the economic arena do not affect the equality of basic liberties. Rawls recognizes that economic inequalities can affect one's ability to *exercise* a liberty; he calls this ability "the worth of liberty."[56] However, though the "worth of liberty" may be affected by economic inequalities, he argues that the liberties themselves can nonetheless be distributed equally.

Daniels retorts: "Equal liberty without equal worth of liberty is a worthless abstraction."[57] Further, he asserts that "our historical experience. . . is that inequalities of wealth and accompanying inequalities in powers tend to produce inequalities of liberty."[58] Moreover, those with more wealth influence political systems and systems of liberty in various ways, e.g., through control of schools. Hence, Daniels asserts, social theory and historical experience suggest that political liberties cannot be separated from economic inequalities in the way Rawls wishes, and those in the original position would not choose principles that assume such a separation.

Related criticisms are levied by Barry and Ackerman. The "lexical ordering" of the two principles appears to require that we would always choose a situation of slightly more equal liberty rather than a situation of greater economic justice. This, Barry suggests, is not likely to be the choice of those in the original position.[59] Ackerman charges that Rawls' "lexical ordering" of the principles reflects a kind of tunnel vision with regard to values: "a program involving the welfare of millions will fail to engage the contractarian's attention, let alone concern, so long as it does not trench upon his precious rights."[60]

The Difference Principle

However, for our purposes it is the difference principle that is central. Many authors consider it to be the core of Rawls' thought. Just as many find it wanting as a principle of justice. The criticisms are so numerous and so varied that only a few can be noted here.

First, assuming the principle is accepted, there are problems of application. How are the "least advantaged" to be identified? Rawls proposes that position and power generally attach to income and wealth, and therefore that income is a sufficient measure. Wolff argues that this is not proven, and Barber and Barry note that Rawls' theory fails to account for racial discrimination or other characteristics not necessarily correlated with income, but correlated with disadvantage in society.[61]

More fundamental are the attacks on "maximin" as a decision strategy. The reasoning behind the difference principle depends on the peculiar features of "maximin." Rawls argues that it is rational for those in the original position to choose such a protective strategy. However, Barber argues that the choice of maximin depends not simply on *rationality*, but on a particular kind of *psychology*, i.e., an un-willingness to take risks.[62] Since those in the original position are not supposed to have a particular temperament, it cannot be presumed that they would be so cautious.

Moreover, the strategy of maximin requires that we care little for what we receive, above a certain minimum; otherwise, we would choose a principle that takes more risk but offers the possibility of larger gain. Nagel argues that this is not "rational" per se: for many life plans, it is precisely the amounts above the minimum that are so crucial.[63]

Hare suggests that the most reasonable response to a situation of uncertainty is not maximin but a strategy called "insufficient reason": where I have insufficient reason to know what position I might hold, I assume that I have *equal chances* of holding any of the possible positions. But in this case, as Rawls admits, the parties would likely choose a principle of average utility as their principle of justice. Rawls excludes "insufficient reason" as a mode of reasoning open to the parties in the original position. Hare charges that he does so, not be-cause rationality requires it, but only to avoid the obvious utilitarian outcome.[64] Responding to the same issue, Wolff suggests that if the parties really cannot estimate the likelihood of their being in any po-sition, then "neither maximin nor any other rule makes the slightest sense."[65]

At least three authors propose that under the conditions of the original position and the veil of ignorance, the choice that would make the most sense is not "maximin" (and hence, the difference principle) but a rule setting a "floor" and then permitting some risk-taking above that floor. The arguments offered for maximin really are good argu-ments for ensuring against calamity, but once a floor is established, those in the original position might choose to take their chances on maximizing their expectations.[66]

Wolff argues further that the difference principle is counterintuitive: why *not* choose a principle that benefitted everyone *except* the least well advantaged?[67] Scanlon points out that the difference principle does not deal with the situation where the position of the least-well-off group is not improved, but the number of persons in that group is reduced.[68] Miller proposes that the difference principle would involve too many "strains of commitment" for capitalists at the top, and hence would not be chosen by those in the original position, who must worry about whether the principles chosen can be adhered to without undue stress.[69]

All these arguments suggest that Rawls has not adequately defended the choice of the difference principle, or perhaps that his principle needs yet other modifications.

Most crucial, of course, are the arguments asserting that the difference principle is not *fair*. Barry argues that there is nothing in the difference principle itself that would prevent a distribution of goods according to race.[70] Thus, it does not offhand avoid violations of some of our most deeply held convictions about justice.

Others argue that it is not fair to those "on top." Just as utilitarianism appears to permit the sacrifice of some for the sake of others, so does the difference principle: those at the top may receive benefits only if those at the bottom do so as well. Nozick's criticism is the most biting here. First, he argues that goods are not "manna from heaven" but products of a productive process.[71] Nozick argues that precisely because the "utility surplus" that can be created through special incentives involves additional effort on the part of some, they are entitled to part of that utility surplus. The surplus cannot simply be distributed as though no one deserved any part of it. The difference principle, which looks only at relative levels of income rather than at contribution to the productive process, appears to ignore these important questions.[72] Indeed, he argues that those on the bottom of the social scale already receive the greatest advantages from social cooperation, and that it would be absurd to suggest that justice requires they be given any more.[73]

Second, Nozick proposes that we imagine the best-off saying to the worst-off, "Look, you gain from this cooperative venture; therefore, we will participate only if we get as much as possible." If these terms seem "outrageous," suggests Nozick, then surely the difference principle is also outrageous, for this is exactly what it requires, in reverse![74] In short, the difference principle appears to violate a Kantian norm and to use some people as means to others' ends. The fact that it uses those better off to help those worse off does not make it any more "just" than a utilitarian scheme that uses the worse-off to benefit the better-off.

Rawls might respond that those who are better-off also gain from the social venture. However, as Sandel notes, this response seems to depend on the notion that talents are "owned" by the community, and this notion is not substantiated, nor does it concur with the individualistic bases of Rawls' theory.[75]

Reiman defends the difference principle at this point.[76] He acknowledges that at first glance this principle does not appear to allow "only reciprocal advantages," as Rawls claims. However, he proposes that if distributions are understood in terms of labor rather than goods or money, the difference principle is not only defensible but indeed would be chosen over free market or other principles.

Reiman's basic argument is this: the social product gained by cooperative venture is really the product of different people's labor. Thus, when "goods" are distributed, what is really being distributed are the proportions in which individuals work for each other. The question of just distribution is therefore the question of reasonable terms for the exchange of labor. When, for example, is it reasonable to exchange t hours of A's labor for $t + n$ hours of B's labor?

Clearly, the answer is: when B receives more than she would by a direct exchange of $t + n$ hours. Thus, if A can be induced to turn out 24 loaves of bread in 8 hours by being given 16 cups of sugar in return, then even if it takes B 16 hours to produce the sugar, B is getting more bread than she would at a straight one-unit-per-hour rate (i.e., B gets 24 loaves instead of 16 loaves). Seen in this light, suggests Reiman, the difference principle does not "confiscate" A's goods and give them to B, but merely prevents A from taking B's (greater) labor without giving B anything in return. Thus, it does not require "sacrifice" from A nor "use" A as Nozick would claim, but merely prevents A from exploiting B's labor.

However, others find the difference principle unjust not to those on top but to those "on the bottom." The notion that normal operations of the market benefit those on the bottom through a chain connection with benefits at the top is a "living fossil," charges Barry.[77] Rawls argues that gross inequalities will not happen between the top and bottom layers; however, Fishkin notes that there is no adequate empirical base for ruling out such a possibility.[78]

Justification

Finally, questions and challenges are raised about the justification for the two principles of justice.

Some challenge whether Rawls has really adopted pure procedural justice, in which the procedure determines the result. Wolff suggests that if Rawls truly used pure procedural justice he could not claim to know in advance what principles would be chosen. Thus, the choice of two principles undermines Rawls' claim to pure procedural justice.[79] Lyons asserts that Rawls *does* have an independent standard of justice—the standard of "fairness" that is built into the original position.[80]

In essence, this amounts to a challenge that the premises grounding the original position are not as "weak" as Rawls claims. Others join in this challenge. For example, Sandel asks why Rawls considers "mutual disinterest" a weak assumption.[81] He argues that Rawls' theory ultimately rests on a particular understanding of human nature—the invulnerable self who always stands apart from his or her experiences. This is not a "weak" assumption. The charge that Rawls manipulates the original situation so as to get his chosen principles also undermines his claims for pure procedural justice.

Others question whether "pure procedural justice" is itself a fallacious theory. The fact that principles are *chosen,* even under fair circumstances, does not necessarily mean that they are *just.* Dworkin notes, for instance, that my (autonomous, fair) agreement to sell a painting for $100 on Monday does not make that a fair price on Wednesday when I discover that the painting is a masterpiece.[82] As Sandel puts it, "If the parties to the original contract *choose* the principles of justice, what is to say that they have chosen *rightly?*"[83] He notes that traditional contract theorists turned to natural law to provide an independent standard. But this, of course, is precisely what Rawls does not want to do. He wants the principles to be fair simply because they are the outcome of rational choice under certain conditions.

Indeed, Lyons proposes that Rawls does have an independent standard. His principles are a rational departure from egalitarianism. But then it seems as though strict equality is the real standard of justice, and Rawls' principles are an "amalgam of a moral egalitarianism and a non-moral acceptance of beneficial inequalities."[84] In short, being chosen in the original position is not synonymous with being just.[85]

Of course, Rawls might respond to this that the choices made in the original position are to be tested against our considered convictions. The requirement of coherence between the principles chosen and our ordinary judgments is the second check and balance for the justice of the principles. This claim also is challenged.

Hare asserts that Rawls simply uses his own intuitions as a check and balance. "Since the theoretical structure is tailored at every point to fit Rawls' intuitions, it is hardly surprising that its normative consequences fit them too."[86] Because of the intuitive elements that enter into such a test, Lyons proposes that it can never be conclusive.[87] Several critics charge that the coherence test and the notion of pure procedural justice are not only a strange juxtaposition, but indeed contradictory: if the theory is pure procedural justice, why should a coherence test be needed at all? And if the principles are justified by their coherence with our considered convictions, why should we need the elaborate mechanism of the original position? These two parts of Rawls' theory do not seem well integrated at the level of justification of his principles.[88]

Finally, some critics charge that Rawls' theory is apolitical, ahistorical, and lacking in the kind of empirical data that would be needed to test out the implications of the principles and provide a genuine check with our considered convictions. As Wolff puts it, "the empirical specificity needed to lend any plausibility to it [is]. . . drained away."[89]

Assessment

Nevertheless, in spite of all the criticisms raised—or perhaps precisely because so much scholarly time and energy has been devoted to analyzing and responding to this theory—A Theory of Justice promises to leave a lasting legacy. Like the utilitarian theory to which it responds, it raises fundamental challenges and sets the agenda for the next generation of reflections on distributive justice. As one of Rawls' staunchest critics puts it, "It is a mark of John Rawls' achievement that I must begin with a critique of contractarian theory."[90]

Wolff proposes that "the real value of a philosophical position lies almost entirely in the depth, the penetration, and the power of its central insight."[91] In this regard, Rawls' theory appears to have two central insights, corresponding to the two parts of the theory: its contract method, and its principles.[92] Each raises a fundamental challenge and future agenda.

Is it possible to construct a theory of justice that does not presume a single good or end for humankind? Where utilitarians posited happiness, or some balance of pleasure and pain, as the good that formed the ground of justice, Rawls' method is intended to derive principles for justice without asserting any single goal and without making justice dependent upon that goal. Such an attempt would appear to be increasingly important in a pluralistic world where different goods are posited by different people. If the method works, it offers the possibility of an approach to justice that depends only on human freedom, equality, and rationality. While critics may consider these "strong" assumptions, they are assumptions sufficiently widely shared today to offer the hope of a common grounding for justice.[93]

Moreover, if Rawls' movement from method to principles works, or if the principles themselves are accepted, then this common ground for justice would appear to require protections for the least advantaged in society. While critics may find fault with the reasoning used to formulate Rawls' principles, the challenge raised by those principles to any future theory of justice is their stress on the position of the least advantaged. The requirements of equal rights, and of only those social and economic inequalities that make the least advantaged better off than they would have been otherwise, provides a standard that can be used to judge social policy and has a strong intuitive appeal to many in our contemporary world.

Thus, whether one takes the "power" of Rawls' central insight to reside in his contractarian method, or in his elaboration of the two principles that protect the least advantaged, it is clear that this theory is sufficiently powerful to set a future agenda for some time to come. It certainly set the agenda for Robert Nozick, who differs with Rawls not only in method but most particularly in understanding the substance of justice.

Three

An Entitlement Alternative: Robert Nozick

If Rawls is right, and justice requires that the basic structures of society be arranged so as to benefit the least advantaged, then a sufficiently strong state will be required to accomplish this end. Indeed, something akin to a modern democratic "welfare" state is envisioned. It is this vision of a strong state that sets the stage for Robert Nozick's alternative proposal in *Anarchy, State, and Utopia*.[1]

Justice is not Nozick's dominant concern. His intent is to argue for a limited role for the state. He wants to show that the minimal state— and *only* the minimal state—is justifiable.[2] Questions of justice arise because distributive justice such as that envisioned by Rawls is often cited as a rationale for the more-than-minimal state. In attempting to show that distributive justice does not provide a rationale for a more-than-minimal state, Nozick offers an intriguing and quite distinctive approach to justice. He calls it an "entitlement" view.

The Role of the State

To see how this theory develops, we must begin with the legitimacy of the minimal state—and the minimal state *only*. Nozick takes a Kantian view that "individuals are ends and not merely means."[3] Individuals are ends in themselves, possessed of certain "natural" rights. This means that there are *constraints* ("side constraints") on action: no actions are permitted that violate fundamental human rights.[4] Thus, for Nozick, a limited set of near absolute rights constitutes the foundation of morality.[5]

Among these fundamental rights is the right not to be killed or assaulted. No one may be "sacrificed" for others. One of the constraints on action brought about by the inviolability of human rights is therefore a prohibition on aggression against another.[6]

But such a prohibition raises interesting questions about the role of the state. If the state becomes the exacter of justice, then it seems to violate this constraint on aggression.[7] This is the anarchist's challenge: the anarchist argues that *any* state violates individual rights. Against this charge, Nozick argues that a minimal state would come into existence by an "invisible hand" process that does not violate individual rights.[8]

In essence, the argument looks something like this: In a Lockean state of nature, the natural law would not provide for all contingencies where human rights conflict: "private and personal enforcement of one's rights. . .leads to feuds. . . . And there is no firm way to *settle* such a dispute."[9] Self-interested and rational persons would therefore form protective agencies to help adjudicate conflicting claims and to make sure that their claims were protected.[10] One such protective agency will tend to become dominant in a territory.

This dominant agency is not yet a state, because it does not claim monopoly on who may legitimately use force to settle disputes nor does it protect all within its territory.[11] However, once the transition is made to include both these elements, then we arrive at the minimal state.[12] How, then, does a dominant protective agency move to acquire a monopoly over force and to protect all within its territory?

When a protective agency is dominant but does not have a monopoly over a territory, problems arise between it and "independent" agencies within the territory. How are "border crossings" to be adjudicated? Nozick's argument here takes the form of procedural concerns about border crossings between those under the care of a dominant protective agency and the independents who are not under its care but nonetheless inhabit its territory.[13]

In such circumstances, a dominant agency would be tempted either to prohibit all border crossings or to permit all border crossings so long as the person was adequately compensated.[14] But neither of these responses will do.

Permitting all border crossings so long as the person is compensated is not an acceptable alternative, for several reasons. First, it puts the "buyer" (or border crosser) in charge: nothing is safe from confiscation, so long as compensation is paid. This raises anxiety. Moreover, some injuries may not be compensable (e.g., death). Thus, to permit all border crossings so long as there is compensation would simply raise too many fears.[15]

Then it seems that the dominant protective agency would attempt to enforce a total ban on all border crossings. But such a ban is not realistic, for it, too, will raise many fears and uncertainties. It is not always possible to avoid crossing a border, and not always possible to negotiate consent beforehand. Thus, some border crossings must be permitted, even where there is no consent.[16]

But once again, this possibility raises the issue of compensation. Remembering that we begin from a position of individual rights—and particularly rights to freedom of action and rights against aggression—the key ingredient in Nozick's theory becomes a *principle of compensation*.

Nozick suggests that there are two places where compensation must be given. One is where an unconsented crossing is permitted. In this case, the person whose boundaries are transgressed without consent is to be compensated for his loss.

However, the second case where compensation is required is equally, if not more, important. It is where a ban is instituted and border crossings are prohibited simply because they *might* be harmful to someone. In this case, one's liberty (to cross boundaries) has been infringed. The person whose action is forbidden because it might be dangerous to others, but where it has not been proven to be so, is to be compensated for the loss of freedom to act.[17]

Thus, both permitting and prohibiting border crossings can give rise to situations requiring compensation. This is a procedural principle for Nozick. To this principle of compensation for loss of freedom Nozick adds one more procedural consideration: one does not have a right to do something unless one knows certain facts. Specifically, one cannot punish a transgressor unless one is sure the person *is* a transgressor.[18]

But now consider the following dilemma for dominant protective agencies. What should the dominant protective agency in a territory do if it deems the procedures for enforcing rights used by independents in the territory not to be sufficiently reliable? Putting together the principle of compensation and the procedural requirement for knowledge, we arrive at an answer. On grounds that the independent agency does not have a right to punish unless its knowledge is adequate, the dominant agency can legitimately prohibit an independent from such punishment or enforcement of borders.

But then the dominant agency has restricted the independent's freedom simply because of a *chance* that its insufficient knowledge will result in harm to others. The principle of compensation therefore requires that the dominant agency compensate the independent for the disadvantages it suffers because of this restriction.[19] The least expensive way to compensate them is to provide protective services to them.

Thus, we arrive at the dominant protective agency protecting all in its territory and claiming a monopoly in that territory on the legitimate use of force.[20] These were the two conditions necessary for the minimal state, and thus we have arrived at the minimal state.

This minimal state arises through the natural process of the formation of a dominant protective agency coupled with principles of compensation and adequate knowledge. Hence, the minimal state arises through an "invisible hand" process resting on minimal principles and containing no immoral maneuvers. It is therefore legitimate, contrary to the anarchist's claim.

Moreover, Nozick argues that this "minimal state" is not only defensible, but exciting. Nozick rejects the idea that there is a single way of life that would constitute utopia for everyone. Since people are so different, a single utopian vision would be absurd. The minimal state leaves people free to form utopian communities within the overall framework without having their rights violated. "Treating us with respect by respecting our rights, it allows us. . . to choose our life and to realize our ends. . . aided by the voluntary cooperation of other individuals possessing the same dignity."[21] The minimal state therefore provides a "framework" for utopia.[22]

We have arrived, then, at the justification for the minimal state. Such a state does not violate anyone's rights, since it arises by an "invisible hand" process coupled with a fundamental moral principle of compensation for loss of freedom. But it remains to establish that only the minimal state is justifiable. Here is where Nozick develops his understanding of justice.

Distributive Justice

At first glance, Nozick's minimal state appears to be "redistributive." It redistributes goods by compelling some people to pay for the protection of others. This suggests that perhaps the grounds have been laid for a broader approach to distributive justice: "If some redistribution is legitimate in order to protect everyone, why is redistribution not legitimate for other attractive and desirable purposes as well?"[23]

However, Nozick argues that the minimal state is *not* redistributive. Its actions are justified not by principles of redistribution of goods but only by the principle of compensation (coupled with the "invisible hand" process).[24] Thus, no grounds have been established by which the state may take from some persons in order to *assist* others. As yet, the door has not been opened to considerations of redistribution of goods on grounds of justice. The minimal state arises through the operation of "negative" rights of nonintervention and related principles of compensation and knowledge; it does not arise through nor imply any "positive" rights of citizens to support by the state.

But is a more extensive state justified in order to provide such support or to achieve distributive justice? Both Rawls and the utilitarians would legitimate a more-than-minimal state in order to ensure that goods are distributed justly—either to protect the least advantaged or to ensure the greatest overall good. Is such a more-than-minimal state entailed by considerations of justice?

Nozick's answer to this question is a resounding no. The pattern of distribution of goods in society, argues Nozick, is not the result of some central agency which distributes everything. Rather, it is the result of myriads of individual exchanges, gifts, and decisions.[25] Lacking such a central distributive or allocative agency, there can be no question of "distributive justice." Instead, we merely have patterns of individual holdings. Hence the question is posed more accurately as a question of "justice in holdings."[26]

When are a person's holdings just? Nozick's answer takes the form of one basic principle: *whatever arises from a just situation by just steps is just.*[27] Picture any original set of holdings or distribution of goods that seems just, e.g., an equal distribution of goods to each person. Then permit people to make choices about exchanging those goods and about giving to each other from their share.

For example, suppose everyone wants to watch Wilt Chamberlain play basketball, and they are willing to give him $1 each for the pleasure of watching him play.[28] Each exchange of $1 to Chamberlain is itself fair. After some time, however, holdings will no longer be equal: Chamberlain will be far richer than everyone else. Yet this discrepancy in holdings is just, says Nozick, since the holdings arise by fair means from an initially just situation. Any attempt to redistribute goods according to some end-goal or pattern (e.g., Rawls' difference principle) must therefore intrude on these free decisions made by people.[29]

Justice in holdings, then, is comprised of the justice of the original acquisition and the justice of the transfers made.[30] This system might be referred to as the principle "from each as they choose; to each as they are chosen."[31] Nozick calls it a "historical" theory, because justice is determined by how the distribution came about, not by what the distribution is.[32]

Indeed, Nozick rejects all "patterned" principles of justice that distribute goods in accord with some chosen "end-state"—e.g., equality of holdings, bettering the position of the least advantaged—or along dimensions suggested by formulae such as "to each according to need" or "to each according to merit." Such principles look only at *what* the final distribution is and ignore the *manner* by which the distribution came into effect.

In contrast to such patterned principles, says Nozick, "*historical principles* of justice hold that past circumstances or actions of people can create differential entitlements or differential deserts to things."[33] Hence, his is an "entitlement" theory. Justice is determined not by the pattern of the final outcome of distribution, but by whether "entitlements" are honored.

Since transfers made in an entitlement system are often done for reasons—e.g., I exchange with others because they will benefit me— "strands of patterns will run through it."[34] That is, the actual distribution will look in part as though it were done on the basis of some formula such as "give to each according to their contributions." But the overall system is not patterned according to any such formulae, but is simply based on the procedural principles of fair acquisition and fair transfer.

Private ownership is the key assumption here. One of the few "positive" rights that Nozick permits as a fundamental human right is the right to acquire and transfer property.[35] Nozick does not elaborate a full theory for fair acquisition and transfer. In general, he seems to support the underlying assumptions of market exchange.

He does accept, however, a "Lockean proviso" on the justice of original acquisition: I am free to acquire by "mixing my labor" with something, *provided* I do not hurt others in the process. Hence, it is not just for me to acquire something that is so limited that my acquisition of it worsens others' condition.[36]

This reasoning about original *acquisition,* suggests Nozick, applies by extension to *transfer* and *purchase.* It would not be just for me to transfer or purchase something so limited that its concentration in the hands of one and its absence to others hurts their situation.[37] "Each owner's title to his holding includes the historical shadow of the Lockean proviso on appropriation."[38] In short, at the root of this system appears to lie a *prohibition against harm* to others deriving from their (Kantian) rights as human beings. One has the right to own goods, but not when that ownership harms others.

However, Nozick gives several interesting twists to the "Lockean proviso." For example, instead of remaining firm on the notion that one may not acquire severely limited goods, he argues that one may indeed acquire them so long as one compensates others so that their situation is not worsened.[39] He argues that a scientist has the right to horde a new compound that she has invented. While there may be some who need the compound in order to live, creating the compound did not *worsen* their state from what it was before. Thus, the scientist is not under any obligation to give or sell the compound, and may exchange it at any price the market will bear.[40]

The notion of what it means to "harm" or "worsen" someone's situation is therefore very central to this theory. Nozick acknowledges that a full theory of justice in holdings needs both a baseline for determining what it means to "harm" others or to make them worse off, and also a theory of property rights.[41]

This approach to justice puts individual liberty and choice in a primary position over any claims for equality of holdings. Indeed, one of Nozick's strongest criticisms of "patterned principles" such as Rawls' difference principle is that they inevitably involve violations of freedom of choice. Since they force arrangements that redistribute the goods that people have chosen to give or exchange, they violate the fundamental Kantian principle of respect for people's autonomy of choice.[42]

One of the interesting implications of this approach is Nozick's understanding of taxes. Taxes, he declares, are equivalent to forced labor.[43] Paying taxes is like being forced to work *n* hours for someone else. Hence, patterned principles of distributive justice that require taxation (e.g., in order to benefit the least advantaged) are "appropriating" or "seizing" people's labor.[44] To seize another's labor is to use that other as a means, not respecting them as an end in themselves. Taxes violate Kantian "side constraints" and are not morally permissible.

The net result of this reasoning is that no justification can be offered for a more-than-minimal state on grounds that it is necessary to ensure distributive justice. Justice is not "distributive" but depends on just acquisition and transfer of holdings. Freedom of choice is violated by any state or system that imposes "patterns" of "redistribution" or attempts to achieve any "end-state" of allocation of goods. "If the set of holdings is properly generated, there is no argument for a more extensive state based upon distributive justice."[45]

Review

In short, Nozick begins with a minimal state based on a minimal set of fundamental (Kantian) rights: rights against injury by others, rights to freedom of choice and action, and rights to own private property. The state has legitimacy only to ensure protection of these rights and compensation for their violation. Where Rawls sees the necessity for societal principles to ensure just distribution, Nozick rejects any role for the state in "distributive justice." Justice is limited to the "commutative" sphere of individual exchanges.

Hence, "justice" for Nozick consists in fair exchange. Justice makes no substantive claims, but consists only in procedural requirements for fairness in exchange. One cannot argue that "justice" requires any particular distribution of goods. Whatever distribution of goods results from free choice and exchange is "just" so long as the beginning point and the exchange itself are fair.

Significantly, justice does not consist in promoting the greatest good of the greatest number, nor in protecting the least advantaged. Neither society as a whole nor any individual or group can make claims against the state for a distribution of goods other than that which arises from free exchanges among individuals. It may be "unfortunate" that some are wealthier than others, but it is not "unfair," provided the rules for free choice in exchange have not been violated.

Critique

The implications of Nozick's theory are startling. Not only does it imply, as he suggests, that taxes are a form of forced labor, but it also sets no "utility floor" or bottom to the plight of those worst off, it requires no limits on the disparity between rich and poor, and it provides no protections against a decline in overall welfare.[46] Thus, clearly it already stands in tension with utilitarian concerns for maximizing welfare and with Rawlsian concerns for protecting the disadvantaged. As one critic puts it, "so long as rights are not violated it matters not for [Nozick's] morality. . . how a social system actually works, how individuals fare under it. . . or what misery or inequalities it produces."[47] But this does not necessarily make it wrong.

Indeed, Nozick would argue that both the utilitarians and Rawls have misunderstood the nature of justice. Though Rawls claims to offer a "pure procedural justice," Nozick charges that in fact he winds up with an "end-state" approach. Nozick's own "historical" view, in contrast, does give a "pure procedural justice"—whatever the end result is, it is just so long as it arose from procedures that are themselves just. As for the utilitarians, they clearly permit the possibility that one person's rights are to be sacrificed for the good of others. This is a violation of Kantian principles of respect for persons.[48]

Does Nozick then offer a more defensible liberal approach to justice? I shall not deal here with those who would argue that any theory of justice must include at least a principle of need or of desert in addition to Nozick's principle of free choice.[49] Rather, I will focus on criticisms raised about his central claims: the historical nature of principles of justice, the centrality of liberty, and the "Lockean proviso" on the justice of holdings.

According to Fishkin, Nozick's approach can be viewed as "protecting 'capitalist acts between consenting adults.' "[50] That is, Nozick begins with assumptions about the right to own private property and to exchange it within certain boundaries of free and knowledgeable consent. Nozick admits his belief that "the free operation of a market system will not actually run afoul of the Lockean proviso."[51]

But these assumptions raise several questions. First, why should property rights have such an "absolute, permanent, exclusive, inheritable and unmodifiable" character?[52] The right to own property is not a "negative" right against interference, but a "positive" right. Nozick offers no arguments for limiting the range of positive rights to those of acquisition and transfer of property. He assumes the legitimacy of private ownership as part of the "state of nature," but never justifies it.

Moreover, property rights entail limitations on freedom. Liberals, suggest Cohen, "see the freedom which is intrinsic to capitalism, but they do not notice the unfreedom which necessarily accompanies it."[53] There are two "freedoms" which might be associated with property: the freedom to own it, and the freedom to use it. "Freedom to buy and sell belongs to capitalism's inmost nature. Other freedoms do not. . . ."[54] Thus, argues Cohen, my freedom to *own* property is always accompanied by limitations on others' freedom to *use* that property. Hence, private property distributes freedom *and* unfreedom.[55] My "positive" right to own property, therefore, is bought only at the price of interference with others' freedom to use it.

But surely Nozick would argue that such interference is justified. The nonowner remains free from "unjustified" interference. This is what Cohen calls the "moralized" definition of liberty. But once we permit such "moralized" definitions that distinguish between justified and nonjustified interference with liberty, we have undermined the grounds for arguments against taxation and social services. To be sure, such things may limit my "liberty"; but they may do so only in a "justified" way.[56]

In short, one must distinguish types of interference with liberty. Hart concurs. Indeed, he suggests that much of Nozick's argument rests on the use of value-laden metaphors, e.g., calling taxation "forced labor," as though there were no difference between restrictions on income and restrictions on physical freedom. Taking account of the gravity of restrictions on different liberties and their importance for the conduct of a meaningful life, argues Hart, will undermine Nozick's claim that all restrictions on liberty violate the separateness of persons.[57]

Moreover, a number of critics raise questions about Nozick's central claims regarding justice in exchange and transfer. His theory depends on the notion that market exchanges, so long as they are genuinely "free" and do not violate fair procedure, result in just outcomes. Nozick assumes that if distribution D1 is fair and we move from D1 to distribution D2 through a process of free choice, then D2 is also fair. But is this necessarily the case?

Here, we might begin by noting that Nozick provides no historical data regarding market systems and their operations. He claims that market systems do not violate the Lockean proviso. But, as we shall see in the last chapter, many liberation theologians offer evidence for consistent violations of that proviso in market systems. Nozick acknowledges the need for principles of rectification of injustice, but does not deal with their actual operation in society.

Many critics suggest that Nozick ignores important aspects of market mechanisms and social cohesion. Ackerman argues that Nozick's basic rights, such as ownership of property, are absolute only in an ideal world, and not in the real world we inhabit. "Nozick's position is dialogically indefensible in a world deeply scarred by illegitimate domination."[58]

Walzer also argues that market exchange is problematic as a basis for justice. He proposes that there are different "spheres" of life; market exchange is acceptable as the basis for justice within certain spheres, but not in all. There are "blocked exchanges"—things that money cannot and should not be able to buy, such as human life. The problem, however, is that "money is insidious, and market relations are expansive."[59] Thus money, far from being the "neutral" medium through which fair exchanges can be worked out, is in practice a dominant good: "money seeps across all boundaries—this is the primary form of illegal immigration."[60]

What both of these authors point to is the fact that in the real world, under circumstances of domination and exploitation, exchange is never as just or neutral as it needs to be in order to support Nozick's theory.

This point is well elaborated by Jon Gunnemann.[61] Gunnemann takes seriously Nozick's argument for the importance of individual exchanges. A market economy is characterized by exchange. Therefore, the justice of a market economy is characterized by justice in exchange—commutative justice, not distributive justice per se. Nozick is correct, therefore, insofar as he points to the importance of exchanges and to commutative instead of (or in addition to) distributive justice.

However, Nozick has failed to take sufficiently seriously the implications of commutative justice. Following Adam Smith, suggests Gunnemann, the root notion in commutative justice is avoidance of harm. Nozick appears to acknowledge this, but does not draw out its implications for the market arena. Harm is avoided by guaranteeing the equivalence of exchange. This requires shared social meanings and equal competence to evaluate the items to be exchanged.

Shared social meaning and equal competence to evaluate the worth of exchanges require a face-to-face encounter and a shared cultural experience. Indeed, Adam Smith thought that exchanges were "unjust" when they involved the extraordinary profits that are gained by distance, secrecy, or other distortions of mutual knowledgeability. Such face-to-face encounters are typical of some market societies, claims Gunnemann, but not of modern capitalistic market systems.

Nozick talks as though we operate in a simple market economy characterized by face-to-face encounter. However, our economy is not characterized by face-to-face encounter, but by capitalist systems that depend on accumulation of capital and on great distance between seller and purchaser. The Wilt Chamberlain example is therefore "deceptive," suggests Gunnemann. No one who purchased tickets for the basketball game had any *direct* dealings with Chamberlain. Tickets are sold by a large agency. Media attention "hypes" the game. Without the trappings of capitalist market systems, it is very unlikely that Chamberlain would develop the kind of notoriety that makes everyone want to watch him play, or that he could indeed become much richer than others.

In short, modern capitalist market societies are not characterized by the circumstances that make for fair exchange and not-harming, but rather exactly by the reverse. Any theory of justice in exchange must take these factors seriously, as Nozick fails to do.

For instance, free and knowledgeable exchange requires access to information. As Ackerman suggests, this raises serious questions about the justice of new technologies, such as television and computer link-ups, which are generally rather expensive. Ackerman concludes that "laissez-faire will systematically give some people special transactional advantages to exploit ignorance. . . ."[62] Walzer concurs: "A radically laissez-faire economy would be like a totalitarian state, invading every other sphere, dominating every other distributive process."[63] Many years ago, Emil Brunner pointed out that "exchange, if left to itself, generates phenomena which destroy free exchange, among others economic monopolies."[64]

Langan also notes that Nozick ignores the large public inputs into the productive process that make private decisions inappropriate as a basc for justice in production and exchange.[65] Individuals do not simply create and exchange goods. "All property is acquired under conditions which the acquirer has not himself created."[66] Nozick ignores the extent to which all transactions are protected and promoted by the community—and hence, the extent to which the community has a "partial right to private property which it claims, for instance, in the form of taxes."[67] Taxes arc not "forced labor" but rather a recognition of the community's contribution to and proper share of the earnings of the individual.

In sum, these critics claim that Nozick's proposal for just holdings arising from freedom of choice is not realistic. Nozick ignores some of the complexities of modern society that make his simple norms of commutative exchange inadequate.

Moreover, Nozick draws many of his examples from the private—indeed from the intimate—sphere. For example, to argue that those who are not chosen have no reason for complaint, he uses the choice of a marriage partner as an example.[68] The example seems suspect at best, since the arena of romantic love is not one in which we usually think issues of distributive justice apply. Minimally, Walzer would say that Nozick is inappropriately using norms from one distributive sphere to apply to another.[69] Fishkin charges that the extension of assumptions from one arena to the other requires a more elaborate theory of the benchmarks for assessing harm in each.[70]

This raises yet another question for Nozick: his understanding of human community and human nature. Hart proposes that "meaningful life" requires not simply protection of liberty but access to the resources and opportunities needed to exercise that liberty.[71] Galston attacks Nozick's approach to the researcher who synthesizes a new drug. Nozick claims that the researcher has no obligations to others to distribute the drug, since he has not made their situation worse off than it was before. Galston proposes, however, that Nozick misunderstands the fundamental point of the "Lockean proviso": it is intended to ensure that no one is prevented from fulfilling basic needs as a result of another's actions. Hence, since the researcher prevents others from fulfilling basic needs—needs for life itself—he is "as culpable as the person who appropriates the last water hole and refuses to share it."[72]

Similarly, Langan charges that while Nozick correctly captures the importance of claims based on specific actions and agreements, he "ignores the possibility of our being bound by ties of natural duty."[73] This is another way of saying that Nozick appears to have a truncated notion of human community. Here Walzer offers a strong critique: he proposes that human society does not arise, as Nozick would have it, merely out of the need for mutual protection. Rather, government arises out of cultural endeavors: "Individuals. . . will necessarily seek out other individuals for the sake of collective provision. They need too much from one another—not only material goods, which might be provided through a system of free exchange, but material goods that have, so to speak, a moral and cultural shape."[74] By limiting the origins of the state to the need for defense alone, Nozick already limits his notions of human nature and therefore of the possibilities for justice.

Assessment

It appears, then, that there are serious problems with this approach to justice in its present form. Nozick himself has pointed to some of the work that would be needed in order to complete the theory: an understanding of private property, and a theory of harms. In addition, his critics suggest that there are serious underlying issues to be considered: the adequacy of his notion of human nature, and of the norms for simple exchange in a complex capitalist society.

Nonetheless, Nozick's liberal challenge will leave an important legacy for those concerned with justice. First, his stress on the *historical* nature of justice is important. Justice does have to do with entitlements as well as with end-states. The utilitarian concern for overall good and the Rawlsian concern for the plight of the least advantaged may be necessary components of a theory of justice, but any such theory must also account for the claims and entitlements created by human activity. This Nozick attempts to do.

As an ideal, his theory surely captures something that is important to justice. If an original distribution is fair, and if all subsequent exchanges are fair, then there is at least a prima facie case for thinking that the final distribution is itself fair. Whether there are other mitigating factors must, of course, be considered. Nonetheless, many of the cries of "injustice" raised today focus on the unfairness either of an original distribution of goods or of exchanges made—treaties with Native American tribes unjustly broken, lands unjustly appropriated from Japanese Americans during the Second World War, and others. The focus of these cries of injustice on issues of acquisition and exchange gives force to Nozick's basic notion of justice in holdings through fair exchange.

Another important contribution of Nozick's theory is to point us squarely to the problem of liberty and its incompatibility with equality. As Fishkin notes, contemporary liberals tend to uphold three values that exist in uneasy tension: merit, equality of life chances, and the autonomy of the family. It is not clear that these values are compatible: liberty exercised by the family (e.g., through decisions about inheritance) always threatens to make life chances unequal and hence to undermine fair opportunity and other procedural underpinnings of liberal theory.[75] If liberty is the primary value, then equality may have to be sacrificed. If equality is upheld, there will be violations of liberty. These trade-offs are clearly perceived by Nozick.

And yet Nozick's limiting of claims or entitlements to "negative rights" against intervention does not fulfil what many take to be the demands of justice. Most of those who see claims as central to justice include within those claims not only negative entitlements based on free choice, but also entitlements based on need, desert, and other elements seemingly ignored by Nozick's theory.[76]

It is to one such approach that we turn next. As we do so, the reader will note some other striking transitions as well. For we are about to leave the arena of philosophy and enter that of theology. Not only do the substantive proposals change, but the sources and modes of reasoning used change as well. We turn then to see what a Catholic perspective on justice might be.

Four

A Catholic Response: The National Conference of Catholic Bishops

In November 1985, the National Conference of Catholic Bishops in the United States released the second draft of a pastoral letter on "Catholic Social Teaching and the U.S. Economy."[1] In this letter the bishops attempt to give "serious and sustained attention to economic justice."[2] The letter therefore presents one Catholic approach to social and distributive justice.

The bishops are responding to many of the same contemporary concerns as are addressed by philosophers John Rawls and Robert Nozick. Indeed, they share with Robert Nozick a fundamental affirmation that humans have rights that cannot be violated. But there the similarity ends. Where Nozick takes this affirmation as grounds for a minimal theory of the state and an argument against any "distributive justice" broader than strict commutative exchange, Catholic tradition has increasingly affirmed the necessity for a broad understanding of justice that goes beyond commutative exchange into "distributive" and "social" justice.

Moreover, as we shift from philosophical reasoning toward the appropriation of a faith stance as the grounds for a theory of justice, the reader will note some changes in style and mode as well. Mill, Rawls, and Nozick all approach justice with the philosopher's interest in conceptual and analytic categories. We enter now an arena focused more directly on social problems and concrete issues of justice. The language and categories—as well as the substantive conclusions—will differ.

66

Since the bishops' letter applies "Catholic social teaching" to the U.S. economy, a quick review of several aspects of Catholic social teaching will set the stage for reviewing the bishops' approach to economic justice.[3]

Catholic Social Teaching

Modern Catholic tradition on "social teachings" begins in 1891 with Pope Leo XIII's encyclical *Rerum Novarum*. It includes subsequent papal encyclicals, conciliar documents, and other efforts to provide a systematic, normative theory relating faith to concrete social conditions.[4]

During this century of "social teachings," Catholic tradition has changed greatly.[5] The changes are both general and specific. On the general level, there has been a shift from a "natural law" approach that assumed human reason could derive absolute answers for social problems toward a recognition of the historical conditioning of all human consciousness, including reason.[6] Concomitantly, there is a movement toward increasing use of Scripture as a base for social teachings. On the specific level, the tradition has gone from arguing that private property must be "preserved inviolate" to arguing that, under certain conditions, lands can be justifiably expropriated.[7] In the midst of such radical changes, it is difficult to present this tradition as a unity.

And yet, a unity it is. Certain philosophical and theological affirmations have remained constant within methodological and substantive flux. While those affirmations do not result in a static and unchanging interpretation of the social situation, they do yield a striking continuity at the level of moral principles, and hence of understanding the demands of justice.

The Catholic tradition on social teachings is rooted in three basic affirmations: (1) the inviolable dignity of the human person, (2) the essentially social nature of human beings, and (3) the belief that the abundance of nature and of social living is given for all people.[8]

It is the dignity of the person "created in God's image" that sets the stage.[9] From Leo XIII in 1891 through John Paul II in 1981, the transcendental worth of persons is the foundation on which social structures must be built. People are prior to institutions and institutions exist for the sake of people. People have rights which neither the state nor any institution may infringe.

Thus, from the earliest days of Catholic social teaching, the popes have consistently rejected any economic system that denies the rights of workers or treats them without dignity. As early as 1891, Leo XIII rejected the "free contract" as the basis for a fair wage. "Natural justice," he argued, requires that the worker receive adequate support, not merely what might be forthcoming in a contract.[10] Leo began a long tradition of rejecting "contract" in favor of a "living" or "family" wage.[11]

In later years, the rejection of contract was extended to a rejection of the market system and hence of capitalist and liberal ideology. "The proper ordering of economic affairs cannot be left to free competition alone," declared Pius XI.[12] Noting that economic supremacy had taken the place of free competition, he flatly declared that "free competition is dead."[13] Paul VI spelled out the reasoning: "if the positions of the contracting parties are too unequal, the consent of the parties does not suffice to guarantee the justice of their contract." And he made explicit the implied judgment on liberalism: "One must recognize that it is the fundamental principle of liberalism, as the rule for commercial exchange, which is questioned here."[14]

By 1971, the Synod of Bishops spoke not merely about the injustice of the contract or market system, but about an entire "network of domination, oppression and abuses." It exposed as a "myth" the assumption that economic development alone will help the poor.[15] The focus was no longer simply on wage justice, but on *participation* in the system. The tradition has long supported the right of workers to form unions.[16] Pius XI had suggested that wage contracts should, "when possible," be modified to include a "contract of partnership" that would permit wage earners to become owners.[17]

Thus began a tradition of linking economic justice with issues of participation and political rights. Noting that the dignity of persons includes the whole person, not just economic well-being, John XXIII argued for social as well as economic development.[18] Following this lead, Vatican II (1962–1965) stressed broad representation of people at every level of decision about economic issues.[19] Paul VI continued the trend by declaring that development must be "integral," promoting the good of the whole person and the good of every person.[20] He noted the legitimacy of both "the aspiration to equality and the aspiration to participation."[21]

In short, economic injustices have come to be linked with political and "participatory" rights. The dignity of persons requires not only treating them justly in the determination of wages, but also according them their full measure of total human rights.[22] An economic system that produces large quantities of goods and distributes them fairly will nonetheless be "unjust" if its organization and structure are such that "the human dignity of workers is compromised, or their sense of responsibility is weakened, or their freedom of action is removed."[23]

In the movement from a stress on wage justice to a stress on "participation," the notion of individual worth and dignity has been increasingly linked to the social nature of human beings. Rights are not simply claims to be attributed to individuals apart from community. Because human beings are social by their very nature, human dignity will be addressed in social relationships. "Justice" is not simply a matter of proper distribution of goods (distributive justice) but also of permitting and indeed requiring each person to participate in the production of those goods (social justice).

Thus, concrete historical manifestations of social institutions become an important arena for the expression of human dignity, and human dignity is tied up with the "common good." Nowhere is this better illustrated than in the tradition's handling of questions of ownership and use of property.

The right to own property has been consistently affirmed since the time of Leo XIII. This is a right "conferred by nature" and necessary for the development of the person, e.g., for fulfilling family duties.[24] At the same time, the *use* of property has always been understood to be directed by considerations of the common good. "The just ownership of money is distinct from the just use of money," declared Leo XIII.[25] He therefore urged the wealthy to share their goods as a matter of "charity."[26] For Pius XI and the succeeding tradition, however, sharing is not a matter of charity but of *justice,* and the state may intervene to set limits on the use of private property.[27]

While the tradition has therefore affirmed a right to private property based on the dignity of the person, it has also defended limits on that right based on the common good. In recent decades, it has begun to justify limited circumstances in which private property may be expropriated by others. *Gaudium et Spes* reports the consensus of Vatican II that "a person. . . in extreme necessity. . . has the right to take from the riches of others" to meet basic needs.[28] Paul VI extends this to the expropriation of landed estates that are not well used or that bring hardship to people.[29] The underlying principle is that all creation is given for humankind; therefore each has the right to basic necessities and "all other rights whatsoever, including those of property and of free commerce, are to be subordinated to this principle."[30]

The common good affects not only the legitimacy of ownership, but also the determination of wages. The right to a "living wage" is always put within the context of the common good: "the wage scale must be regulated with a view to the economic welfare of the whole people."[31] Distributive justice in the area of wages therefore becomes a complicated matter of balancing workers' rights and contribution with the requirements of the community, including the impact of wage scales on employment rates.[32] Nonetheless, the tradition affirms the priority of labor over capital.[33]

Perhaps most striking in the tradition is its consistent concern for the plight of the poor. In Leo XIII and Pius XI are found the roots of a tradition that perceives the mere *fact* of inequality of wealth as a sign of injustice. The poor, declares Leo, do not deserve their plight. Rather, "a very few and exceedingly rich. . . have laid a yoke almost of slavery on the unnumbered masses of non-owning workers."[34] Pius XI asserts that the immense numbers of poor, on the one hand, and the superabundant riches of the few, on the other, are "an unanswerable argument" that goods are "far from rightly distributed and equitably shared."[35] John XXIII argues that there is "manifest injustice" in placing a whole group of citizens (farmers) "in an inferior economic and social status, with less purchasing power than required for a decent livelihood."[36] Vatican II declares that "excessive economic and social differences. . . militate against social justice. . . ."[37] The "uplifting of the proletariat," as Pius XI called it, was a constant theme during this time, and was applied both within cultures and between wealthy First-World and poor Third-World countries.[38] These concerns culminate in what is today called the "option for the poor": "true relationships of justice and equality," declares Paul VI, require "the preferential respect due to the poor."[39]

The grounds for this option, however, have changed. From Leo XIII through John XXIII, the special position of the poor is justified largely on grounds of reason: the poor are not able to fend for themselves; therefore, distributive justice requires that the state take particular care of them.[40] Phrases such as "justice and equity require" are common, but the terms are rarely defined.[41] The reader is left to be persuaded by the logic of the argument. This is the more traditional "natural law" approach and is summarized in the statement from *Gaudium et Spes* that the church "has worked out these principles [of justice and equity] as right reason demanded."[42]

Since the time of Vatican II, however, with increasing consciousness of the historically conditioned nature of human reason, church leaders have turned increasingly to Scripture as the justifying ground for the "option for the poor." In *Justice in the World*, the Synod of Bishops spelled out God's preference for the poor in both Old and New Testaments.[43] Paul VI reiterated that "we are instructed by the Gospel" in the proper respect for the poor.[44]

It is also important to note that the tradition has worked on a model of social consensus. Labor and capital need each other; thus, classes are not in opposition to each other and harmony is possible.[45] In spite of its concern for the poor and its growing emphasis on the priority of labor and the right to participation and political involvement, the tradition has shied away from any suggestion that revolution will be necessary in order to secure the rights of the poor. The vision of justice is a vision grounded in a sense of solidarity, mutual responsibility, and joint benefit. Individual rights and the common good are never in opposition to each other but are mutually supporting basic principles. Similarly, reason and revelation are mutually supporting sources of insight.

The Bishops' Letter

The heritage of this tradition shows strongly in the bishops' letter on the U.S. economy. The dignity of the person, the social nature of humankind, the special position of the poor, stress on participation, assumptions of social consensus, the rejection of "rigid" capitalism[46]— all are present. And they are combined with an effort to provide a more systematic treatment of justice, drawing on tradition, scripture, and philosophical reasoning.

The bishops declare that the fundamental criterion for assessing the economic system is its impact on human dignity: *"The dignity of the human person, realized in community with others, is the criterion against which all aspects of economic life must be measured."*[47] Thus, moral policies for economic life must be shaped by three questions: what they do *for* people, what they do *to* people, and *how* people *participate* in them.[48]

Since the poor are most affected by economic decisions, and since they have a special claim by virtue of being vulnerable, such decisions must be judged by what they do to and for the poor and by what they enable the poor to do for themselves.[49] The treatment of the poor is the "litmus test" for the justice or injustice of a society.[50] Stress on the position of the poor is supported both by Christian conviction and by "the promise of this nation to secure liberty and justice for all."[51]

Hence, the fundamental moral criterion for all economic policies and decisions is simply: "They must be at the service of *all people, especially the poor*."[52]

Following the post-Vatican II trend, the bishops devote considerable time to developing a scriptural base for this fundamental criterion. While they stress that "philosophical reflection" and "common human experience" confirm these religious convictions, it is the religious convictions themselves that are developed at length.[53]

Israelite tradition provides a theological framework through themes of creation, covenant, and community.[54] The creation stories affirm the "alien dignity" of every human being.[55] They also give us fundamental themes of common use of goods: "From the Patristic period to the present, the Church has affirmed that misuse of the world's resources or appropriation of them by a minority of the world's population betrays the gift of creation since 'whatever belongs to God belongs to all.' "[56]

From the covenant tradition we understand God to be a God of justice. *Justice* in Scripture has several nuances. Most fundamentally, it means a sense of "what is right"—including both ṣedaqah (righteousness) and *mishpat* (right judgment and concrete acts of justice).[57] However, there is a distinctive aspect of the biblical presentation of justice: "the justice of a community is measured by its treatment of the powerless in society."[58]

The New Testament affirms these themes of creation and covenant: Jesus brings a "new creation" and a "new covenant."[59] The new covenant calls for discipleship or service, summed up in the great commandment to love one's neighbor as oneself.[60] In Luke's gospel in particular, the "poor" are blessed and are the objects of God's special love.[61] Thus, the foundation is laid for a "preferential option for the poor."[62]

This scriptural foundation provides a basic vision. It does not yield direct policy imperatives. On the conviction that this vision is "intelligible to those who do not share Christian religious convictions,"[63] the bishops seek an ethical framework drawn from generally accepted norms.

Among these are norms of "basic justice." These norms state minimal levels of mutual care and respect; they are not as all-encompassing as the biblical vision.[64] But they provide a common grounding for judgments about economic justice. Here the bishops draw specifically on the Catholic tradition of commutative, social, and distributive justice.[65]

Commutative justice requires fairness in agreements and exchanges between private parties. It is commutative justice that requires a fair wage and adequate working conditions.[66] *Social* justice requires people to participate in the creation of the common good. It therefore also requires society to enable them to do so.[67] The requirement for full employment, for example, can be drawn from social justice. *Distributive* justice deals with the allocation of social goods. The bishops propose that distributive justice requires special attention to needs, prohibits discrimination, and provides for a minimal welfare floor.[68]

These fundamental requirements of "basic justice" are summarized in a requirement for "*the establishment of minimum levels of participation in the life of the human community for all persons.*"[69] The "ultimate injustice" is for people or groups to be treated as if they were "nonmembers" of the human race.[70] Hence, all people have fundamental human rights as enumerated, for example, in Pope John XXIII's *Pacem in Terris* and in the U.N. *Declaration of Human Rights.*[71]

These convictions also give rise to three priority principles. First, fulfilling the basic needs of the poor is of the highest priority.[72] Second, increasing participation for the marginalized is a high priority.[73] Third, investment policies should be directed to benefiting those who are poor or economically insecure.[74]

These priorities are not economic policies per se, but "norms" against which policies can be judged.[75] The movement from norm to policy is complex, and the bishops do not assert the same moral authority for their policy judgments as for their normative claims.[76] Nonetheless, in view of the importance they attach to labor and to the plight of the poor, a quick review on each of these issues will round out the bishops' understanding of economic justice.

Because of the importance of work for the fulfillment of human life, people have a right to work.[77] Thus, the first specific policy recommendation made by the bishops is a call for "full employment."[78] High levels of unemployment are unacceptable because of their impact on human life.[79] The bishops therefore call for the establishment of a right to work, urging that it is a joint task between private enterprise and government.[80] They propose targeted employment programs, expanding job training, the development of new strategies for job sharing, and other such efforts.[81]

As has become traditional in Catholic social teaching, the bishops walk a line between acceptance and critique of capitalism as the context for work. On the one hand, they support "the freedom of entrepreneurship, business, and finance."[82] At the same time, they follow Catholic tradition in arguing that there is a "social mortgage" on private property.[83] They also contend that the "free market" gives employers greater bargaining power, and therefore that justice requires certain minimal guarantees for workers.[84] Hence, they reject the notion that a free market automatically produces justice.[85]

Employment alone, however, will not solve the problems of poverty given high priority by the bishops. Here, the bishops review statistics and analyses to demonstrate the depth and nature of poverty in the United States.[86] Our economy is "marked by a very uneven distribution of wealth and income."[87] Since Catholic tradition has taken such disparities to represent a form of injustice, the question must be raised whether justice requires equality of wealth and income. To this, the bishops answer no.[88] However, following Catholic tradition, they suggest that there is a "presumption" against extreme inequalities which are detrimental to social solidarity.[89] Such inequalities are therefore to be rectified.

In doing so, the "principle of participation" must be honored.[90] That is, programs that do things "with" the poor are to be preferred to those that do things "for" the poor in a paternalistic manner. The bishops give special attention to problems of stigmatization of poverty.[91] Tax reforms, removing discriminatory barriers, education, and welfare programs are all supported.[92]

Review

Justice, for the bishops, is neither the result of societal consensus nor of rational deduction or calculation alone. It is rooted in a faith tradition that responds to a loving and just God. God's intentions for human life determine what is just and what is unjust.

Hence, the justice or injustice of discrepancies in wealth is not determined by assessing the fairness of the exchanges involved historically. Nor is it determined by principles of autonomous choice or calculations of the greatest overall good. Discrepancies of wealth indicate a situation in which some fail to remember that the goods of the earth are given for use by all; such a situation is unjust because it violates both the social nature of human beings and the purposes for which God gives the riches of the earth.

Because Catholic tradition advocates the common good, at first glance it appears similar to utilitarianism. But the common good means something different from the greatest good of the greatest number. The common good is judged by the plight of the poor; never would the greater good of some justify deprivation of others. Thus, far from justifying abuses of the powerless, the "common good" and the social nature of human beings becomes a corrective against such abuses.

Because Catholic tradition advocates certain "rights" of the individual that are prior to the interests of the state and that cannot be abrogated by the state, at first glance it also appears similar to Nozick. But where Nozick's rights are primarily "negative" rights against interference, Catholic tradition upholds "positive" rights to welfare. One of these is the right to a "living" wage. But acceptance of this right means precisely rejection of the unfettered market exchange system that Nozick lauds. Thus, taking a perspective that advocates individual rights does not yield the same understanding of economic justice.

Because protections for the disadvantaged loom large in the bishops' view, at first glance it also appears that they share much with Rawls. Indeed, substantively they do. The plight of the worst off becomes the measuring stick for the justice of a society. Again, however, this seeming agreement masks numerous underlying differences. The bishops appear to recognize more explicitly than Rawls does that economic differences will result in political inequalities. The grounding for protection of the disadvantaged is very different. For Rawls, protection of the least advantaged is the result of a self-interested calculation under conditions of ignorance; for the bishops, it is the result of acknowledgment of the presence and will of a loving God.

Critique

The second draft of the bishops' letter is too recent for a body of critical materials to have developed around it. However, the first draft of the letter engendered a great deal of controversy, and some criticisms made of that draft are applicable also to the second.

Much of that criticism focused on specific policy applications.[93] Many who criticized the specific policies nonetheless agreed in large part with the bishops' underlying theory of justice.[94] Our focus here is on aspects of both principle and policy that raise issues for the view of justice presented in the pastoral letter.

The first draft was roundly criticized by advocates of the free market system. The bishops' view put too much power in the hands of government and was too costly, critics charged. In their concern for *allocation* of goods, the bishops had ignored the need for *production* of goods and the remarkable successes of the free market system in that regard. Many critics see the economy as a trade-off in which equality of reward must be sacrificed to the incentive systems necessary to spark increased production.[95] Hence, Flanigan argued that discrepancies in wealth are not necessarily a sign of injustice. Rather, they might be the sign of a healthy economy that provides more jobs and has less overall poverty than would an economy characterized by fewer such discrepancies. With more jobs and less overall poverty, the economy is actually more "just."[96]

Novak explicitly linked these concerns to distributive justice. He argued that the bishops failed to discern the moral underpinnings of the market system. The market, he declared, was "designed and promoted" in order to meet 11 criteria of distributive justice, including concern for needs, effort, equality, welfare, incentives, inventiveness, and so on.[97] Thus, in the view of these critics, justice is better served by a relatively unfettered market system than by the interventions proposed by the bishops.

Terms such as *participation* or *marginalization* were castigated as being too vague or inapplicable to the North American situation.[98] Indeed, Novak found unacceptable the use of *participation* as a criterion for justice because it does not easily apply to those whom the bishops note are among the majority of the poor—children, the elderly, and others who cannot fully "participate."[99]

Critics also charged that the bishops' view was "utopian" and ignored the problem of human sinfulness.[100] A realistic assessment of economic justice requires "reflections on ordinary self-interest," Novak insisted.[101] He and others rejected the bishops' focus on "institutionalized" injustice and argued for a perspective taking seriously individual sin and responsibility.[102] In this regard, they found wanting the bishops' use of Scripture, suggesting, for example, that the parable of Lazarus and the rich man is directed to individuals rather than to nations or institutions.[103]

Indeed, the bishops' use of Scripture to provide a base for an "option for the poor" was criticized for not using a sufficiently sophisticated hermeneutic. Poverty in biblical times is not the same as poverty today, Novak contended. Any use of Scripture must attend to such problems of application. He therefore charged the bishops' letter with being "ahistorical" in its use of Scripture and its corresponding view of justice.[104]

Several of these criticisms appear to be addressed in the second draft. For example, Novak's proposed question "What can people do *with* and *for* the poor to *enable* them to take responsibility?" appears to be reflected in the bishops' adoption of the question "What do they [economic structures] enable the poor to do for themselves?"[105] Although the bishops continue to support governmental intervention to provide for the poor, they attempt to make proposals consonant with the market system and they urge the development of a healthy economy as the "first line of attack" against poverty.[106]

Indeed, the second draft appears to water down or draw back from the emphasis on the poor and its implied critique of capitalism in the first draft. The first draft stated boldly that the "fundamental" norm for judging policies and decisions was to be: "*Will this decision or policy help the poor and deprived members of the human community and enable them to become more active participants in economic life?*"[107] While the necessity to judge systems by what they do to the poor is still present in the second draft, the "fundamental" moral criterion has become "the service of *all people, especially the poor.*"[108] This is a slight shift in emphasis, but not unimportant.

Further, it is supported by other shifts in emphasis. In the first draft, the second "priority" principle made clear that the poor had priority over the rich: "*Increased economic participation for the marginalized takes priority over the preservation of privileged concentrations of power, wealth, and income.*"[109] In the second draft, participation for the marginalized is simply "a high priority," not necessarily one that takes precedence over the demands of others.[110]

The sense of a movement away from the genuine perspective of the poor may be reaffirmed by noting some inconsistency between underlying theory and priority principles. The "basic justice" that represents the amalgam of Catholic tradition with philosophical reasoning and human experience is said to be summarized by the demand for "minimum levels of participation."[111] Yet, participation is not listed as the first priority principle. Meeting needs is given first priority, and participation is simply a "high" priority.[112]

Whether these accommodations will satisfy critics on one side of the coin remains to be seen. But they are almost guaranteed to anger critics on the other.

For example, Harrison charged that, at the point of policy, the bishops' first draft operated out of "neoclassical" economics. Neoclassical economic theory supports "utility maximizing" and profit-oriented market systems. Hence, she charged them with inconsistency, arguing that they adopted in practice a perspective that they refuted in theory.[113]

In the second draft, the bishops note that there are "competing views" of how to understand the economy of the United States. One view (Harrison's "neoclassical economics") accepts the fundamental assumptions of capitalism and the free market; the other contends that injustices are inherent "in the very nature of the capitalist system" and therefore argues for the abolition of private property and market systems.[114]

The bishops insist that they follow Catholic social teaching in rejecting both of these ideological extremes.[115] They neither accept the free play of the market, unfettered by government interference, nor do they accept the view that capitalism cannot be reformed but must be replaced. Instead, they adopt the "spirit of American pragmatic tradition" and argue for reforms to the system in light of principles of justice.[116]

The question is whether such a "pragmatic," "reform"-oriented view really represents a fundamental acceptance of capitalist economic principles. To be sure, the bishops reject the notion that a free market automatically produces justice, and they accept limits on private property developed by Catholic social teaching.[117] But nowhere do they offer a structural critique of capitalist systems. Though they deplore the widening gap between rich and poor in the United States, they do not suggest that such a gap is the inevitable outcome of modern capitalism. Nor do they offer fundamental criticisms of liberal tradition that have appeared in Catholic social teachings.

Indeed, they take pains to assure their readers of the complementarity of Catholic and American perspectives.[118] A Catholic respondent to the first draft criticized them for using language and arguments that "could in principle be accepted by the rationality operative in the liberal, American tradition."[119] Thus, far from being too critical of market systems, some critics find the bishops too accommodating to the presuppositions of liberalism and capitalism.[120]

A related challenge has to do with whether the bishops have genuinely taken a "preferential option for the poor." Though the theory of justice propounded gives the poor a special place, Baum charged that the "option for the poor" in the first draft of the letter really amounted to no more than a policy guideline to be *concerned* for the poor. The bishops were still talking *about* the poor rather than *with* or *from* the poor.[121] Another critic noted that "no poor actually speak in these pages." Instead, the roster of those who testified before the bishops "is a roster of the positioned, the powerful, and the credentialled."[122] Similarly, Harrison charged that the analytic perspective failed to deal adequately with the very poor in global perspective.[123]

In this regard, Rasmussen made an important criticism of the use of Scripture in the first draft. The Bible offers two traditions on the poor, he suggests. The Exodus-Sinai legacy sees God as liberator and requires the restructuring of society to overcome poverty. The monarchical-hierarchical legacy sees God as the comforter of the poor within a system where the rich have philanthropic duties to the poor. Both are legitimate biblical strands, argues Rasmussen, but the first is central. The liberation approach to poverty is not well reflected in the bishops' letter.[124]

If an "option for the poor" is understood to imply (1) focusing on structural injustices and oppressions, and (2) accepting liberation as a central category with its implications for principle and policy, then the bishops' second draft also fails to represent a genuine option for the poor.[125] Nowhere does it advocate the "hermeneutic of suspicion" that is being pressed, for example, by liberation theologians.[126] And it contains little explicit emphasis on institutionalized injustice.[127] In short, critics charged that the bishops gave lip service to an "option for the poor" that was not evident in their own work, either procedurally or substantively.

Issues around the adequacy of the bishops' option for the poor lead inexorably to questions regarding their understanding of "social consensus." The bishops stress that the "option for the poor" is not a slogan which "pits one group against another."[128] Here they follow Catholic tradition by refusing to see conflict between the common good and the assertion of rights for some. But is the model of consensus that has undergirded so much of Catholic social teaching an adequate model?

Just as critics on the one side claim that the bishops have not taken sin sufficiently seriously because they have neglected individual sin, so those on the other side would say they have not taken sin sufficiently seriously because they assume too much consensus. Catholic tradition has tended to be more positive about human capacities than has Protestant.[129] The assumption that all can live in harmony is but another evidence of this lingering positive understanding of human life.

A related question is whether principles drawn from a vision of the "common good" that perceives consensus are adequate to the task of addressing an American economy based on principles of self-interest and power politics.[130] When Pope Paul VI challenged each community to "analyze with objectivity the situation which is proper to their own country,"[131] he clearly had in mind precisely what the bishops have done—the application of basic *principles* from the tradition to the particular *situation* of the country. But it is at least legitimate to ask whether such principles are relevant to a situation that seems to have arisen because of the operation of very different principles.[132]

Some additional methodological challenges can be put to the grounding offered for the norms and principles. Cox suggests that the bishops "forged their plea in an effort to appeal to reason" and in so doing may have neglected the important question of appealing to the heart by engaging religious cultures in the United States.[133] Indeed, though the bishops develop scriptural grounding for their norms, they turn to philosophy for the enumeration of "basic justice" and its requirements. There is a jump here. Moreover, they presume that basic justice in the arena of distributive justice requires attention to need; as the first half of this volume indicates, there is no consensus on "need" as the basic requirement of distributive justice in philosophy.

Indeed, the bishops appear to be trying to "have it both ways": to have their faith and their philosophical reason too. The bishops assert several times that "reason and human experience" confirm their theological reflections. But the evidence for this assertion is scanty. Where earlier Catholic tradition depended too much on reason, there is an ironic lack of appeal to reason in this letter. In a passing reference, the bishops note that "many social values" in our affluent culture "are in direct conflict with the gospel vision."[134] But if this is so, then the congruence between reason and revelation needs more substantiation than it has been given.

Assessment

Substantively, the contribution of the bishops' letter must be seen against the background of the changing Catholic tradition on social teachings. The bishops stand well within that tradition when they lift up the joint norms of human dignity and common good. Their stress on the common good keeps human dignity from dissolving into a "rights" language that is purely individualistic.[135] If Rawls has failed to convince us that an "option for the poor" can be derived from self-interested rationality alone, perhaps the bishops provide an additional grounding for this view of justice. Their use of Scripture avoids both the trap of fundamentalist literalism and the trap of a "perfectionist" religious ethic that has nothing to do with everyday life.[136]

At the same time, the "common good" is not simply the "greatest net good" of utilitarian theory. Institutions exist for people, and individuals may not be harmed in order that others may prosper or that the "system" may work. There is a much stronger sense here than in classical utilitarian theory of the ways in which we all need each other for survival and for prosperity. The grounding of common good in God's intentions for the human race keeps that good from being smothered either by individualism or by a "greater number."

In addition, the bishops recognize the importance of economic justice and rights. They give it a primacy missing in Rawls' liberal theory. The movement of Catholic social theory toward "participation" as the root issue for justice provides a link between the economic and the political arenas that appears to be missing in Rawls.

The fundamental challenge provided by the bishops' letter is no doubt how we understand the grounding for our rights and obligations.

Do they emerge out of a self-interested social contract, or out of a vision of a human life of peace and justice intended by a loving God? Is human community merely the product of a need for mutual protection, as Nozick would have it, or is human community a necessary part of the expression of the fullness of human life and personality? The faith stance taken by the bishops clearly supports the latter view.

But then we must raise the profound question of how one speaks out of the faith stance of a particular community to a larger constituency. The bishops hope to keep "reason and revelation" together—to appeal both to Christians and to others in society. They operate out of a long-standing "Catholic conviction that human understanding and religious belief are complementary, not contradictory."[137] But is this true? Some Protestants would certainly charge that faith contradicts "human wisdom"—Christians are called to be "fools" in the eyes of the world. Thus, some would argue that Christians cannot "have it both ways," appealing both to those who share the faith and those outside of it.[138]

But the importance of the bishops' letter for theories of justice lies not only in its substance but also in its method. While the letter ultimately comes "from the top down"—from the bishops to their constituencies—it nonetheless represents several years of data-gathering, collaboration, and an attempt to discern the "signs of the times." It is a group product, not an individual effort. For that very reason, it is sometimes more uncertain about its choices of social theory than it might otherwise be. But it has the advantage of reflecting at least a spectrum of experience and opinion, if not as full a spectrum as many critics would like.

The bishops' method reflects the Catholic tendency to trust in the common good, in reason, and in consensus. We turn now to see what happens when a theory of justice is developed out of distrust rather than trust in human capacities.

Five

A Protestant
Alternative:
Reinhold Niebuhr

During much of the time that Catholic social teachings were developing, American Protestant Christianity was being pushed and prodded by the prodigious works of Reinhold Niebuhr. Like the Catholic tradition during the same period, Niebuhr's own thought underwent considerable change.[1] Nonetheless, a core understanding of justice permeates his long career and provides a significant Protestant alternative to the Catholic view.

Niebuhr respected his Catholic peers, but thought that they, like their liberal counterparts in the philosophical world, were not sufficiently "realistic" about the necessity for struggle in history. Hence, his own "Christian realism" attempts to take seriously the limits of political and social possibilities.

Love and Sin

For Niebuhr, prophetic religion combines an utmost seriousness about history with a transcendent norm. It never permits us to ignore history or to seek escape from it; yet it does not find its ultimate goals or standards within history. Therein lies the special gift of prophetic religion.

In Christianity, Jesus is the "perfect fruit of prophetic religion": he is both in history and points beyond history.[2] Jesus represents seriousness about history (incarnation) and yet a normative realm beyond history (the kingdom). From Jesus, we get the supreme ethical command: love. His ethical ideal is one of complete obedience to God's will.[3] This is perfect love, which Jesus both embodies and commands. For Niebuhr, therefore, Christian ethics begins with love. Love is, first, a derivation of faith. At the same time, love is a "natural" requirement for humans. Individuals can realize themselves only in community, or "brotherhood." The "kingdom of God" indicates our fulfillment in a world of perfect harmony. Love, therefore, is "the primary law" of human nature and the highest principle of Christian ethics.[4]

What is love? Niebuhr distinguishes "mutual" love from "self-sacrificial" love.[5] Mutual love is not simply a calculating reciprocity; it springs from concern for the other. But it is never free from prudential concern for oneself as well. It is therefore never the purest form of love. Self-sacrificial love requires a selfless identification with the needs of the other.[6] It is characterized by "disinterestedness," meaning a lack of self-interest and a concern only for the life and well-being of the other.[7] Its ideal is perfect harmony; its purest expression, self-sacrifice.[8] Hence, for Christians, the cross is the symbol of this ultimate perfection.[9]

If such selflessness were a simple possibility in history, there would be no need for justice, since all would coexist in a perfect harmony of love.[10] Unfortunately, claims Niebuhr, there is no such possibility: "the love commandment stands in juxtaposition to the fact of sin."[11] It is the attempt to be "realistic" about sin that grounds Niebuhr's approach to social ethics. Where Catholic tradition stresses the creation of humans in God's image, Niebuhr stresses another part of the creation story: the fact that humans are "fallen" sinners.

Sin for Niebuhr has two dimensions. The religious dimension of sin is idolatry: "The sin of man is that he seeks to make himself God."[12] We are creatures, but we are constantly tempted to forget that fact and to attempt to be God. A common form of this sin of idolatry is identifying our interests with the general interests, or thinking that our perception of truth is *the* truth.[13]

But sin also has a moral dimension. "The ego which falsely makes itself the centre of existence in its pride and will-to-power inevitably subordinates other life to its will."[14] If perfect love is the sacrifice of self, sin is the assertion of self against others: "sin is always trying to be strong at the expense of someone else."[15] The moral dimension of sin, therefore, is *injustice*—an unwillingness to value the claims of the other or to see one's own claims as equal but not superior to the other's.[16] The root injustice is exploitation: "exploiting, enslaving, or taking advantage of other life."[17]

In the face of these "historical realities" of self-interest and exploitation, sacrificial love is not an adequate social ethic. Its ethical ideal of disinterestedness "is too rigorous and perfect to lend itself to application in the economic and political problems of our day."[18] Niebuhr's constant theme is that a profound faith must appreciate "the recalcitrance of sin on every level."[19] He rails against those who underestimate the power of sin both in individual life and especially in collective life. Even for the individual, a life of selfless giving is impossible.

But when we move from the individual to the collective level, the impossibility of disinterestedness is compounded. For here, the one who would act out of self-sacrifice is sacrificing not only his or her own interests, but the interests of others. Thus, self-sacrifice becomes "unjust betrayal" of the other.[20] Groups, therefore, must never be expected to behave altruistically: "groups have never been unselfish in the slightest degree."[21] This is particularly true of nations: "no nation in history has ever been known to be purely unselfish in its actions."[22] It is also true of classes.[23]

Love remains for Niebuhr an "impossible possibility"—relevant as the ultimate standard by which actions may be judged, but not possible of immediate implementation in the social world. Economic and political affairs must therefore be governed by what Niebuhr calls the "nicely calculated less and more" of justice.[24]

Justice

Justice is for Niebuhr a multifaceted term having something of the character of paradox.[25] Indeed, it might be said that he uses the term rather loosely to cover a plethora of functions. He speaks of the "spirit of justice,"[26] of "rules" and "structures" of justice,[27] of calculating rights,[28] and, most often, of balancing forces or competing interests.[29] He declares that "justice that is only justice is less than justice."[30] To understand these diverse uses of the term and the seeming contradictions involved, one must understand the dialectic of love and justice in Niebuhr's thought.

Perfect justice would be a state of "brotherhood" in which there is no conflict of interests.[31] But such a state is no more possible in the world of sin than is a state of perfect love. Indeed, perfect justice would be love. But since love cannot be fully realized, neither can perfect justice. To be "realistic," justice must assume the continued power of self-interest.[32] In history we live always within the realm of "imperfect" or "relative" justice.[33] It is the inevitability of these relative distinctions in history that is so often ignored by Christian thinkers, says Niebuhr.[34] Relative justice involves the calculation of competing interests, the specification of duties and rights, and the balancing of life forces.

Such relative justice has a dialectical relationship to love. On the one hand, rules of justice extend our obligations toward dealing with complex, continuing, and socially recognized obligations that go far beyond the immediate boundaries of what we would naturally feel for others.[35] In doing so, such rules serve the "spirit of brotherhood" or love. In this sense, then, rules of justice support love and must not be excluded from the domain of love. Complex relations require justice.

Yet, because justice is always relative, it is always capable of improvement. Any historical manifestation or rule of justice could always approximate more closely the ideal of love.[36] Justice is the best *possible* harmony within the conditions created by sin, but it not the best *imaginable* harmony. Indeed, the laws and rules of justice themselves will always reflect the partiality of human perspectives; they are not "unconditionally" just.[37]

Hence, all historical enactments of justice stand under the judgment of love. Love requires justice for the complex realities of the sinful social world. Yet, love also transcends, fulfills, negates, and judges justice. It transcends justice because it goes beyond, exceeding the demands of justice.[38] It fulfills justice because it never implies less than justice: where life affirms life, justice is done.[39] It negates and judges justice because every historical justice is imperfect and stands under the judgment of more perfect possibilities of human community.[40]

This explains why "justice that is only justice is less than justice." The minimal justice of equal rights before the law, for example, is indeed justice. But it never fulfills the total spirit of the willing affirmation of life with life that is required for "perfect justice" or love.

Niebuhr's ethical stance is therefore dualistic, affirming the necessity for norms of both justice and love, neither of which is sufficient in itself.

But what, then, are the requirements of justice? Niebuhr elaborates these in terms of rules or laws (the more "theoretical" side of justice) and in terms of structures.

Rules of justice

Because every historical justice is less than love and is therefore capable of improvement, there are for Niebuhr no universal or absolute standards of justice.[41] Indeed, Niebuhr suggests that any attempt to codify justice—for example, into a listing of rights—always develops into injustice because "the perspective of the strong dictates the conceptions of justice by which the total community operates."[42]

But this does not imply a relativism that acknowledges no standards at all. For Niebuhr, there are generally valid principles that inform and judge historical choices. The two most important of these are freedom and equality.[43]

Freedom is the essence of human nature and therefore always stands as a crucial value. But unfettered freedom in the economic sphere too often means that the poor are priced out of the market.[44] Thus, freedom cannot stand alone as a social principle: it must always be "relegated" to justice, community, and equality.[45]

Equality emerges as Niebuhr's highest standard of justice: "a religion which holds love to be the final law of life stultifies itself if it does not support equal justice as a political and economic approximation of the ideal of love."[46] Equality is the "regulative principle" of justice, a "principle of criticism under which every scheme of justice stands."[47] "Equal justice" is the best approximation of "brotherhood"—or love—under the conditions of sin.[48] Equal justice is therefore "the most rational possible social goal."[49] The rule of equality includes both concerns for process (e.g., impartiality in the calculation of needs) and also for equality as a substantive goal (e.g., equal civil rights).[50]

Even equality, however, can be modified. Indeed, in historical societies, differences of need and social function make inequality a necessity.[51] In addition, "imaginative justice" goes beyond simple equality to note the needs of the neighbor.[52] And equal justice will itself issue in a kind of "option for the poor":

A social conflict which aims at greater equality has a moral justification which must be denied to efforts which aim at the perpetuation of privilege. . . . The oppressed have a higher moral right to challenge their oppressors than these have to maintain their rule by force.[53]

Structures of justice

But how is justice to be established? It is obvious from Niebuhr's elaboration of freedom and equality that reason has a role to play in bringing about justice. It is "constitutive" in the rules of justice.[54] Its canons of consistency will lead us to condemn special privileges that cannot be justified.[55] It enables us to judge things from a more inclusive perspective.[56] It helps provide a penetrating analysis of factors in the social situation.[57] Moreover, it can destroy illusions.[58]

But reason alone cannot bring about justice. First, reason itself is not free from the influence of human passions and interests. Reason, too, is "fallen."[59] All rational estimates of rights and interests are "contingent" and "finite," "tainted" by passion and self-interest.[60] Thus, "even the most rational" of people will propose corrupted definitions of justice.[61] *Our* truth is never *the* truth.[62]

Indeed, Niebuhr suggests that the development of rationality has actually injured the search for social justice by "imparting universal pretensions" to partial social interests.[63] The privileged classes are particularly guilty of this form of sin; they do not realize how much their presumed rational calculations are affected by their economic interests.[64] Indeed, Niebuhr gives a kind of "epistemological privilege" to the oppressed, suggesting that "those who benefit from social injustice are naturally less capable of understanding its real character than those who suffer from it."[65]

It is partly because of the distortions of reason that there can be no universal "rational" standards of justice. It is also for this reason that "neutrality" in social struggle is impossible, and that efforts to remain "neutral" really have the effect of working to the advantage of entrenched interests.[66]

Second, reason alone is not adequate to establish justice because justice involves the totality of human life which includes both reason and passion. The realist knows, claims Niebuhr, that "history is not a simple rational process but a vital one."[67] Justice in history therefore requires not merely rules and principles but the balancing of competing forces, the taming and ordering of human "vitalities."[68]

This is to say that justice requires the use of power or coercion to establish order: "justice is achieved only as some kind of decent equilibrium of power is established."[69] Niebuhr is perhaps best known for his constant stress on the balance of power: "Any justice that the world has ever achieved rests upon some balance between the various interests."[70] This, he declares, is a "clear lesson of history."[71]

This also means that, for Niebuhr, *power* yields injustice. Niebuhr speaks frequently of the injustice of power: "it may be taken as axiomatic that great disproportions of power lead to injustice."[72] Justice in social systems, therefore, is not simply a matter of how goods are distributed, but is also a question of the proper ordering and balancing of power. The struggle for justice is a struggle to increase the power of the victims of injustice.[73]

Political and Economic Implications

Since justice requires a balance of power, the centers of power are crucial to the historical enactment of justice. Two such centers loom large for Niebuhr: the political and the economic.

In response to the threat of fascism, much of Niebuhr's energies went to arguing for and supporting forms of strong democratic government.[74] The "structures of justice" needed for balancing vitalities in society require both a strong organizing power, or government, and a balance of powers.[75] Too little organizing power results in anarchy; too much becomes tyranny.[76] Government must always be understood as both necessary and oppressive.[77]

But government is not the only important center of power. Niebuhr's concern for social justice took root during his pastorate in a church in Detroit; it was the struggles of the workers during hard economic times that set the agenda for his life-long passion.[78] In contemporary society, argues Niebuhr, centers of power are largely economic.[79] In his early years, Niebuhr saw political power as so dependent on economic power that "a just political order is not possible without the reconstruction of the property system."[80] While he later modified this seemingly trenchant Marxism, he never lost his concern about the power of the economic sphere. The diffusion of political power in democracy makes for justice, he declared; yet the political power of the individual does not eliminate "flagrant forms of economic injustice" in capitalist democratic countries.[81]

Thus, economic justice is a prime concern for Niebuhr. Both liberalism and Marxism, Niebuhr charges, fail to understand property as a form of power.[82] Because property is power, "inequalities in possession have always made for an unjust distribution of the common social fund."[83] Niebuhr therefore is a staunch critic of contemporary capitalism, which he finds "a particularly grievous form of social injustice."[84] "Modern capitalism breeds injustice because of the disproportions of economic power that it tolerates and upon which it is based."[85]

Since justice requires a balance of power, Niebuhr asserts early on what Catholic tradition later affirmed: economic justice requires political participation and the use of power.[86] But, for Niebuhr, political participation will be won only by the conflict of force with force. Sinful people will never voluntarily give up their power and self-interest. Justice requires coercion.

Therefore, Niebuhr refused to deny the possibility of revolution or other violent approaches to the establishment of justice. The balance of power that represents justice always involves a tension; tension is covert conflict, and covert conflict can become overt.[87] While Niebuhr often argued on pragmatic grounds against violence, he found no absolute arguments against it in principle: "Once we have made the fateful concession of ethics to politics, and accepted coercion as a necessary instrument of social cohesion, we can make no absolute distinctions between nonviolent and violent types of coercion."[88] Hence, "the fight for justice will always be a fight."[89]

To those who would say, "If only we loved each other violence would not be necessary," Niebuhr would retort that they underestimate that if.[90] To those who advocate nonviolence as the "Christian" way, he would retort that they fail to observe the ways in which they are already involved in violence: "the whole of society is constantly involved in both coercion and violence."[91] For Niebuhr, government especially was a source of injustice and violence: in preserving "peace" it always does so by enforcing certain injustices.[92] Niebuhr rails against modern "robber states" who deny to the poor the very privileges that they have seized for themselves.[93]

In brief, Niebuhr's understanding of justice might be summed up in the phrase "love compromising with sin." Justice is derivative from love, yet distinct from it. The demands of justice are, in the end, the demands of love.[94] Perfect love is a harmony in which human wills are not in conflict. Justice approximates that harmony through norms of equality and liberty. Yet, there can be no absolute rules of justice, since any approximation always stands under the possibility of correction. Justice requires constant attention to the distortions in our perspectives. It also requires the use of coercion to achieve balance of power.

For Niebuhr, the Protestant affirmation of justification by faith alone does not make efforts for justice irrelevant. Rather, it means that "we will not regard the pressures and counterpressures, the tensions, the overt and covert conflicts by which justice is achieved and maintained; as normative in the absolute sense; but neither will we ease our conscience by seeking to escape involvement in them."[95]

Review

Niebuhr's approach to justice differs from all those considered above because of his emphasis on sin. For Niebuhr, sin or conflict among people is a persistent and enduring aspect of human life. Hence, both the utilitarians and the Catholics would be "unrealistic" in assuming a harmony between individual interests and the greater or common good. Rawls' dependence on reason is fallacious, because reason itself is tainted by sin and thus cannot alone yield valid principles of justice. Nozick's trust in the "free" exchanges of market systems ignores the fact that humans will always seek unfair advantage in exchange so that resulting divisions of goods are unjust. In a world permeated by sin, no single principle or approach can yield eternally valid principles of justice.

Instead, justice must be characterized first by a balance of power. The ideal is harmony of self with self; justice approximates this ideal by balancing powers so that the weak are protected against the strong. Such a balance is only a relative harmony, but it is a necessary and just harmony. Even Rawls' first principle of equal liberty would probably not satisfy Niebuhr, since it does not ensure a balance of power between classes. Similarly, Niebuhr would argue contra the bishops that justice does not consist in meeting the needs of the poor but in ensuring that they have enough power to meet their own needs.

But a balance of power is not itself the ideal. Thus, every historical enactment of justice for Niebuhr also involves injustice. Justice is never finished or achieved. Every relative justice is a relative injustice as well. One can never rest satisfied that justice has been done simply because "the greatest good" has been done or the disadvantaged are better off than they were before, or exchanges are fair, or living wages are granted. Each of these forms a part of justice, but each holds within it also a perversion of justice. All structures and arrangements of justice are temporary and partial. They always await the better balance, the closer approximation of the harmony of love that is perfect justice.

Critique

Niebuhr's works have been subjected to long scrutiny. Almost every aspect of his work has been criticized—his theology, his Christology, his factual interpretations of history. And almost every criticism by one party has brought defense of Niebuhr by another. Only those issues immediately relevant to understanding his theory of justice will be addressed here.

Let us begin with the most inclusive criticism: the charge that Niebuhr *has* no theory of justice. Brunner puts it pointedly: "Reinhold Niebuhr has never worked out a clear concept of justice whereby the difference between the demands of justice and those of the supreme ethical norm of love might be understood."[96]

Harland defends Niebuhr at this point. He argues that failure to define a term does not mean that one lacks a clearly articulated concept of it. *Justice* is not defined by Niebuhr, he suggests, because it is a relational term—it has no meaning independent of love.[97] Niebuhr says much the same in responding to his critics: "Justice is an application of the law of love. The rules. . . are applications of the law of love and do not have independence from it."[98]

Nonetheless, there is merit in Brunner's charge. Though it is clear that love and justice are in dialectic relationship for Niebuhr, it is not always clear what this means. Niebuhr tries to walk a tightrope between philosophical and theological definitions of justice. On the one hand, he appears to adopt philosophical definitions of justice—for example, in his advocacy of equality and freedom as basic rules of justice. But not only are these terms never well defined by Niebuhr; they also carry unexamined liberal freight in a theology otherwise critical of liberalism.[99]

On the other hand, the identification of perfect justice with the theological norm of love also raises problems. If the demands of justice are in the end the demands of love, then it would seem that the principles of love and justice should be compatible in substance: whatever justice requires should be what love requires. Niebuhr seems to imply this when he says that love can exceed justice, but never abrogate justice.[100]

But if justice admits the claims of the self while love requires the sacrifice of the self's interests, it is difficult to see how they can always be substantively identical. It seems that self-interest is legitimate for the one and not for the other. This means that, at least in relationships involving the self, love and justice cannot require the same thing. One critic charges that Niebuhr's ethics leaves the Christian caught between two worlds with two ultimate norms, "distraught and divided in all ethical decision."[101]

Niebuhr would no doubt reject this assessment. In a sinful world, love *must* compromise with sin. In a sinful world, self-interest always enters, and justice—the fair promotion of interests—is therefore always needed. Love is ethically purer than justice, but not more valuable socially.[102] Love is not a direct norm for action in the social world. Rather, it functions as a reminder of the ideal of complete harmony and of the need to keep seeking a more perfect resolution to the conflict. Moreover, in a sinful world where all life does not affirm all other life, the sacrifice of the self's interests is the truest expression of the seeking after harmony. Thus, love is appropriate in every negotiation for justice as a leavening force to restrain the exercise of self-interest.[103] Though justice and love are not identical, they are complementary.

Still, the dialectic between love and justice would be clearer if Niebuhr spelled out the requirements of justice in more detail. He does not specify procedures or rules for determining how interests are to be weighed and how to determine what is "due" in justice. This failure begs vital questions, charges Thompson. "What, for instance, does the norm *justice*. . . mean in practical terms?"[104] Does Niebuhr's "realistic"—and ultimately pragmatic—approach amount to nothing more than an idiosyncratic reading of what is "right" in each situation? Even Niebuhr's use of "middle axioms" such as equality and balance of power does not prevent his ethic from being a "more or less intuitive approach to ethical issues," McCann suggests.[105]

Other critics defend Niebuhr at this point. Outka grants that rules of justice are not well elaborated in the theological literature of Niebuhr's generation. He notes nonetheless the validity of Niebuhr's point that all specific rules will not escape the corruptions of ideology and interest. Thus, he says, we must acquiesce to a certain tentativeness in ethics: "particular situations often demand a highly sensitive, *appropriate* response which may render formally preferable principles and rules unhelpful or even distortive."[106] Harland agrees: "Because justice always exists in a dynamic relation between *agape* and the uniqueness of concrete historical situations one can never say 'exactly' what justice is apart from either *agape* or the situation."[107]

However, McCann charges that this leaves Niebuhr with an ethic that fails to illuminate "difficult tactical questions." Niebuhr's middle axioms have only "limited usefulness" as guidelines for social ethics: they "remain intuitive precisely where they should be more explicit."[108] There is in Niebuhr little careful elaboration of the extent to which "justice" means "treatment in accord with needs" or "merit" or "productivity" or some other criterion.[109]

These criticisms reflect Niebuhr's relative lack of systematic theory about justice. Niebuhr's role was often that of the gadfly. His language and style reflected that role: his was the "polemical method of overemphasis"[110] or the "technique of demolition."[111] In a world characterized by gross injustices, Niebuhr's approach is the prophetic technique of exaggeration and excoriation, rather than the philosophical technique of reasoned argument. Note, for example, the value-laden language he uses in describing materialistic theory as an "antidote" for the "toxin of the hypocrisies by which modern society hides its brutalities."[112]

Niebuhr's dialectical approach to love and justice therefore functions more as a cautionary device than as a concrete guideline. Justice requires enough organizing power, but not too much. Justice requires struggle for equality, yet always with the recognition that our understanding of the situation will be wrong. "Justice" for Niebuhr functions more as a principle of prophetic criticism of *any* stance taken than as a precise norm or philosophical category.

Moreover, his theory is dependent on his historical method—what Catholics would call his reading of the "signs of the times." His cautions and decisions on specific social issues are therefore a clue to his understanding of justice. For example, constitutional instruments are required in any international order to "guarantee the weaker nations their rights."[113] The fact that "children do starve and old people freeze to death in the poverty of our cities" is taken as a sign of the violence of structures that constitutes injustice.[114] Equal rights in race relations is the "minimal standard" of justice.[115] The principle of a "living wage" is affirmed, provided it is "generously interpreted"—i.e., coupled with old age insurance and unemployment insurance.[116] Justice requires "equal opportunity of development."[117] The Marxist dictum "to each according to need" stands as an ideal, albeit unworkable.[118] Justifiable inequalities are limited by what is necessary for differentiated social functions.[119]

In fact, some of his criticisms are quite pointed. The idea that the profits of industry are a reward for the sacrifices made by owners may have had merit in the early days of capitalism, he declares, but does not hold in a day when concentrations of capital mean that few "sacrifices" in luxury are made by investors.[120] The issue has become, not simply "fair distribution" of property, but whether the right of property is legitimate at all.[121] The success of free enterprise in the United States has been due to certain natural and historical factors (e.g., wealth of resources) that make it not a good model for other places.[122] As always in Niebuhr, it is "history" that teaches us and provides the ethical insight.

Then it becomes important to ask whether Niebuhr reads history correctly. Here, Herbert Edwards charges that Niebuhr was very much a "white man of his times." In dealing with racial justice, for example, Niebuhr too easily adopted the view of white southerners and urged patience for blacks. Though equality was his moral ideal of justice, that ideal was subject to compromise with the "realities" of a situation read through the eyes of a white power structure that saw black efforts for justice as divisive.[123] Similarly, M. M. Thomas argues that Niebuhr misread the political and moral dynamics of the non-Western world and therefore came to stress issues of political justice in disregard of other questions of justice.[124] Feminists have also criticized Niebuhr for ignoring the particular injustices faced by women. Where "sin" for men may be represented by the will to power over others, some feminists argue that sin for women has more often been a too-ready self-effacement.[125] Some commentators would charge that his reading of history is too affected by his own theological presuppositions. Many have taken him to task for overemphasizing sin and failing to lift up human potentialities for good. Here Outka is bold in his critique. Niebuhr, he says, "makes the situation of incompatible interests the paradigm of moral reflection within 'historical society.' But this is a mistake. For the interests of [people] are by and large more complementary than conflicting."[126]

Since Niebuhr's understanding of justice is based directly on his assessment of the centrality and persistence of sin in human life, this criticism has import for assessing Niebuhr's approach to justice. If sin is less pervasive than Niebuhr assumes, there would be more possibilities for the direct application of the norm of love to social issues, or for the closer approximation of justice to the ideals of "brotherhood" and harmony.

Other critics, however, support Niebuhr on this point. Bennett asserts that "nothing has happened to refute the realistic analysis of the stubbornness of evil in society."[127] Indeed, one critic suggests that, far from being too pessimistic, Niebuhr is too optimistic about human potential.[128]

Related to the question of whether Niebuhr overestimates sin is the question whether he underestimates the role of love or of reason in social ethics. That is, does Niebuhr underestimate religious and rational sources for social ethics?

Here, the critique of John Howard Yoder is probably most important.[129] Yoder views Niebuhr as providing the "classic" statement of an approach to ethics that makes Jesus irrelevant.[130] In his view, Niebuhr's approach to love and justice amounts to a "concession that Jesus is really on the other side from one's own."[131] That is, if Jesus' ethic is a pure ethic of love, but such an ethic cannot be applied in the world, then whatever ethic we do apply—such as "justice"—is clearly in contradiction to Jesus. For Yoder, therefore, Niebuhr's ethic would not be Christian. Yoder argues for the direct relevance of the norm of love to the social arena. Far from arguing that we need separate or distinct norms of "justice" to deal with political issues, Yoder suggests that Jesus gives us a "political" ethic in the application of the cross to the political arena.[132]

Niebuhr would no doubt have respected Yoder's pacifism as an expression of the ideal of love. But he would perhaps have charged that such pacifism ignores the "violence" that is being done all the time precisely in political structures: no one can avow an ethic of pure love "from the vantage point of privilege and security."[133] Moreover, Yoder may not appreciate the extent to which Christians remain sinners and cannot know the will of God in the social arena.[134]

However, this suggested retort raises additional problems for Niebuhr's own theory of justice. For, if all knowledge is corrupted by one's own social location and historical age, then surely Niebuhr claims too much finality for his own interpretations of Scripture and for their social implications. Wieman charges that Niebuhr "corrects the Bible according to his own convictions."[135] Burtt simply accuses him of reflecting "the limited standpoint of Protestant Christianity."[136]

For instance, Niebuhr's identification of Jesus' ethic with an ethic of pure "love" and "disinterestedness" is anathema to other Christians. Herzog charges that in separating a "religious" ethic of love from a "rational" ethic of justice, "God in Christ is completely removed from the immediate claims of justice."[137] Similarly, Gamwell argues that if personal fulfillment means self-sacrificial love, which cannot be realized in history, then Niebuhr has ultimately moved out of the realm of history and thereby undermines his own professed interest in it.[138]

Although it was always Niebuhr's intention to expose the limitations and fallacies in any perspective, he may have failed to see some of his own. McCann suggests that Niebuhr and his followers in "Christian Realism" failed to sustain the paradox of his own vision. Niebuhr's advocacy of democracy as the best form of government led him to support "developmentalism" in the so-called Third World.[139] His view of human nature was based on aggressive personalities and on their form of sin: will to power. This may not be the form of sin most expressed by oppressed peoples.[140]

Assessment

What is Niebuhr's contribution to a theory of justice? The legacy of Reinhold Niebuhr to the field of ethics is a strong one. Stone declares that "the best starting place for the serious student of social ethics is Reinhold Niebuhr's thought."[141] Gustafson considers *The Nature and Destiny of Man* "the most important American contribution to Protestant theological ethics in the first half of this century"[142] Heschel goes even further in his praise: "In boldness of penetration, depth of insight, fullness of vision and comprehensiveness, Reinhold Niebuhr's system excels everything which the whole of American theology has hitherto produced."[143]

However, these comments are directed at Niebuhr's work overall—his theology, his social ethics, his interpretations of American religious behavior. That he was a significant political voice during much of this century is not in question. But what are the contributions of his theory of justice?

Here, Niebuhr's greatest weaknesses may also be his greatest strengths. Critics appear to find fault with Niebuhr at two fundamental points where justice is concerned: his lack of clear definition and rules for justice, and his (over) emphasis on sin and the necessity for struggle and balance of power. Yet it is precisely these two that provide a significant contribution to any theory of justice.

Where Nozick claims to offer a historical theory of justice, yet fails to peruse history, Niebuhr begins with the injustices of history. As one critic puts it, Niebuhr "asked the right questions." [144] He takes seriously the historical realities of conflict as well as cooperation. He is the "unveiler par excellence of human sin in its blatant and subtle forms." [145] In contrast to the philosophical theories outlined in this volume, and in contrast to much of Catholic tradition, Niebuhr's strength lies in his stress on the realities of conflicting interest. If "justice" has to do with competing claims, as Hume and most of his followers have thought, then a theory of justice must take seriously that competition. This Niebuhr does.

Particularly important in this regard is his perception of the distortions built into rational explanation and justification. Critics of John Rawls noted that his attempt to find a "neutral rationality" on which a theory of justice could be based ultimately fails, because his own definition of the original position carries value assumptions and biases within it. Niebuhr would have predicted this. He cautioned against all attempts to trust too much in our own rationality or our own perceptions.

To be sure, in his suspicion of human rationality and his consciousness of the ubiquity of sin, he leaves an ethical system without clear rules and definitions. But this very fact, hailed by critics as a weakness, may also be a strength. Niebuhr's paradoxical and dialectical approach to justice is unsatisfying for those who seek clear definitions and proposals. Yet it may come closer to truth than efforts to find a single criterion for justice, whether "the greatest good of the greatest number," the position of the "least advantaged," or the fairness of exchange.

Niebuhr leaves no one with an easy conscience that "justice" has been achieved simply because the poor are now a bit better off than they were before, because industrial systems are more efficient, or because exchanges have been handled fairly. Niebuhr gives no criteria by which we can be assured that "justice" has been done. Indeed, we can never be so assured, precisely because every historical enactment of justice is also an enactment of injustice. Niebuhr's overriding goal was always to caution against the pride that attends any security about our political programs. Humility about our programs and achievements and openness to consider alternatives that might be more just would have salutary effects in some powerful circles.

Yet, this very tendency to distrust any human efforts or programs raises, as we have seen, a crucial question: How does one know? If all reason is suspect, then whence comes knowledge? It is this question that becomes the probing ground of liberation theology, and to which we turn in the next chapter. Stone suggests that Niebuhr's thought "needed the influence of being brought closer to the passionate fires of revolution in the Third World."[146] Those passionate fires suggest a different understanding of justice.

Six

A Liberation Challenge: Jose Porfirio Miranda

Like Reinhold Niebuhr, liberation theologians stress the reality of conflict in society. Like Niebuhr, they argue for sin—and hence for justice—to be understood as *structural* phenomena. And like Niebuhr, they emphasize the importance and meaning of history. And yet "Christian realism" and "liberation theology" have come to be understood as opposing camps in the theological world. For all of the similarities, a different—and quite distinctive—view of justice emerges from liberation theology.

A sustained attempt to provide a theory of justice from the liberation perspective is Jose Porfirio Miranda's *Marx and the Bible*.[1] However, because this work consists largely of scriptural exegesis, I will both set the stage for it and supplement it by drawing on the liberation approach more generally. In particular, I will draw heavily on the work of Gustavo Gutierrez, who is acknowledged as one of the first theologians to have given shape to the liberation approach.[2] It should be remembered, however, that liberation theology is not solely a Latin American phenomenon. It is also important to remember that it is largely a spoken, not written, theology; it has an elusive character difficult to render with vitality on paper.[3]

A New Method

"God chose from birth to live the same as the poorest, didn't he?. . . [H]e was born poor and wants us all to be poor. Isn't that so? or rather, he wants us all to be equal."[4]

These words spoken by a poor woman in Latin America make an appropriate place to begin an examination of liberation theology, for liberation theology is first and foremost a new *method* for doing theology. "Latin American theology does not start with existing theologies but with the real and concrete totality of what is taking place."[5] It starts with "praxis"—with passionate and committed involvement in the struggle for liberation.[6] It is a dialectical reflection: reflecting on practice in the light of faith and on faith in the light of practice.[7] Theology is therefore the "second movement," after involvement.

Moreover, this involvement has a clear bias: the perspective of the poor and oppressed. Its beginning place is the perspective of the poor. "The theology of liberation is an attempt to understand the faith from within the concrete historical, liberating, and subversive praxis of the poor of this world—the exploited classes, despised ethnic groups, and marginalized cultures."[8] The "poor" are variously defined. The term is used both literally and in an extended meaning that applies not only to those who are materially deprived but also to those who are "marginated" in society, lacking full access to and participation in socioeconomic and political processes. Thus, the "poor" include laborers, peasants, the elderly and young, the unemployed, women, those from oppressed ethnic and racial groups, and others.[9] These people have become, in Gutierrez's words, "nonpersons," "suffering misery and exploitation, deprived of the most elemental human rights, scarcely aware that they are human beings at all."[10]

Thus, two important circumstances set the stage for liberation theology: first, the realities of poverty and oppression, and second, the commitment of Christians to the struggle for liberation.[11] In the Latin American context, the two elements of oppression and struggle for liberation are sharply defined.[12]

Latin America is characterized by oppression, repression, and dependence. The realities of oppression—"untenable circumstances of poverty, alienation and exploitation"[13]—are everywhere evident: "It leaps out at you. It is impossible not to see it."[14] Former colonialization has simply been replaced by new forms of oppression. Internationalization of capitalism and proliferation of multinational corporations has resulted in a situation in which Third World countries have relatively little power or autonomy in the bargaining process; if they refuse to provide the desired cheap labor, corporations simply go elsewhere. Military regimes and "national security states" have arisen to ensure compliance of the masses with this economic agenda. The gap between rich and poor is growing.[15] Scholarship in the social sciences confirms that Latin America has been "from the beginning and constitutively" dependent.[16] Thus Dussel calls colonial domination the "original sin" of the prevailing world system.[17]

Based on their involvement in these realities, many Christians and church leaders have denounced the grave social injustices in Latin America.[18] They have also formed "comunidades eclesiales de base"— small grass-roots organizations that educate and raise consciousness about social justice issues.[19] As a result of these activities, Christians in Latin America have suffered persecution.[20] To economic poverty is added political repression. Such persecution merely reinforces the perception of the deep social ills plaguing Latin America.

Thus, liberation theology refuses "to conceal the conflictive nature of society under the cloak of generic, innocent-looking terminology."[21] Social conflict implies class struggle: history today is characterized by a division "into oppressors and oppressed, into owners of the means of production and those dispossessed of the fruit of their work, into antagonistic social classes."[22] Hence, "only a class analysis will enable us to see what is really involved in the opposition between oppressed countries and dominant peoples."[23] Here, most liberation theologians turn explicitly to Marxist analysis of class conflict.

Such an analysis implies the need for a paradigm adequate to the situation of dependence. "Development" will not do, since it implies no conflict. Gutierrez excoriates those who fail to perceive that lack of equitable distribution of goods is not simply an "unfortunate" circumstance that will be overcome in time, but is "the fault of the system itself."[24] In a situation characterized not by "underdevelopment" but by oppression, "liberation" is the proper paradigm. "The concerns of the so-called Third World countries revolve around the social injustice-justice axis, or, in concrete terms, the oppression-liberation axis."[25]

Recognizing the realities of dependence, oppression, and repression, Christians who have joined the struggle for liberation are calling for new interpretations of Scripture and new bases for Christian ethics. Too often, theology has been a tool justifying oppression.[26] From the "praxis" perspective, Christians argue that "salvation" is not simply a "spiritual" phenomenon, but is a unitary concept that includes social justice as well as spiritual well-being. Liberation implies social revolution, not merely reform.[27] Its goal is the creation of a "new person" in a "new society."[28] Nor is "sin" to be understood as an individual, internal phenomenon: "Latin American theology does not start. . . with a relationship of the solitary self with another individual self but considers the structure in which the sin of the world conditions our own personal sin."[29]

Out of their perspective of involvement in liberation struggles, liberation theologians no longer trust mainline (European-dominated) readings of either the situation or of Scripture. They have developed a "hermeneutic of suspicion."[30]

Thus, for example, they seek not the "balance of power" lauded by Niebuhr, but a transfer of power.[31] And "violence" must be understood differently: the violence of the subjugator is evil, while the violence used by those who seek liberation from oppression is not.[32] No general judgments against violence can be levied, but only judgments from within the "praxis" seeking liberation. Liberation theology is thus contextual in its ethics.

Out of these commitments and reflections emerges a new kind of rationality—"the rationality of a concrete, historical undertaking."[33] This rationality dares to posit the vision of a social revolution that others find "utopian." Gutierrez charges that these "dominators" of the system simply are not familiar with the scientific rigor and rationality of concrete theology. Praxis gives a perception of aspects of the Christian message that escapes other approaches.[34] Dominant among these is an understanding of the central biblical concern for justice.

Justice

Above all, Christians involved in liberating praxis are gleaning from Scripture and praxis a new understanding of justice. In the Bible they find eloquent testimony to God's concern for the poor and oppressed and evidence for a view of salvation that includes the struggle for a just society as part of salvation history.[35] In particular, they find that Scripture is clear that to know and to love God is to do justice for our neighbor.[36]

Miranda's analysis reflects several aspects typical of liberation theology: he begins with injustice; he uses Marxist analysis to develop perspective on the situation; he finds capitalism as a system to be a core locus of injustice; he finds agreeable sources within Christian (in his case, Catholic) tradition; and he turns to Scripture for confirmation of the centrality of justice and the condemnation of injustice.[37]

Liberation theology starts with prophetic denunciation of "the grave injustices rampant in Latin America."[38] To understand what "justice" is and what it demands, one begins with a review of those injustices experienced by the oppressed. Liberation theology presents in the first place, therefore, *a theory of injustice.* "In the underdeveloped countries one starts with a rejection of the existing situation, considered as fundamentally unjust and dehumanizing."[39]

A number of terms emerge as descriptions of injustice in the situation of the oppressed: slavery, humiliation, exploitation, repression—and, above all, poverty itself.[40]

But "injustice" is not simply a condition or circumstance. It is structured and institutionalized. It is *systematized.* The misery and exploitation of the poor do not just "happen." They are due "not to 'neglect' but to the very logic of the system."[41] The existence of the poor is "not politically neutral, and it is not ethically innocent. The poor are a by-product of the system in which we live."[42] Thus, the cry for liberation and justice is an attack on the entire system or social order, not merely on isolated instances of injustice. "More than anything else, it is the system itself that is being called into question by the exploited."[43]

Particularly crucial here is the capitalist system that undergirds the modern "security states" in Latin America. For Miranda, "capitalist oppression carries with it the weight of thousands of years of injustice and hardening of hearts and obstinacy of spirit."[44] The issue, therefore, is not simply to weed out injustices within the system, but to change the system itself: "it is a question not only of attacking the prevailing distribution of ownership, but the very right of differentiating ownership, especially of the means of production."[45] Noting that whether capitalism rises or languishes, "the outlook for the poor is dismal," Gutierrez also argues that capitalism is "of its very nature" detrimental to the poor.[46]

Miranda draws explicitly on Catholic social tradition to ground his judgment on the "injustice" of the situation in Mexico.[47] Leo XIII's great encyclical *Rerum Novarum* argued for the right of workers to contract freely for wages. But it also noted that workers accept harder conditions than they should because they are victims of force and injustice—i.e., because they have no alternative. Justice presumes some freedom of choice; the fact that something is chosen or agreed to does not mean that it is "just."

Miranda suggests that the same logic be applied on the macroeconomic level. Where 75% of a population receives only one-third of the national income, we can presume that the "choices" that led to this situation were not altogether voluntary. "No one would say that the workers freely accept the national system of contracts and transactions in virtue of which they are kept in a state of perpetual disempowerment and the capitalists in a perpetual situation of privilege."[48] The justice of a wage system depends on the supposition of free choice. But the "violence" of the system forces capitulation: "the man has no choice but to accept or to die of hunger."[49] Thus the prevailing distribution is due to injustice.[50]

Since the distribution of ownership is simply the accumulated distribution of income, private ownership of the means of production is the result of this coercive distribution of income—i.e., it is the result of injustice.[51] Moreover, Miranda argues that this kind of "differentiating ownership" that divides people into classes could not come to be without a system of violence and spoliation: "the accumulation of capital in a few hands could not and cannot be achieved without an institutional violence exercised over wages and prices."[52] Private ownership as we know it therefore is "robbery—legalized, institutionalized, civilized, canonized robbery."[53] Dussel makes a similar argument: I have a right to what I work for, he suggests, "and it is always relatively little. If I have a lot, it is because I robbed someone."[54]

It is for this reason, declares Miranda, that both the Bible and the early church fathers understood "almsgiving" to be "justice." In the Bible, this act is not a supererogatory "charity" but "a restitution that someone makes for something that is not his."[55] As one early church father put it, "You are not making a gift of your possessions to the poor person. *You are handing over to him what is his.*"[56] Thus, suggests Miranda, the Bible confirms what can also be seen from economic study: the kind of private ownership that differentiates rich from poor is unacquirable without violence and spoliation.[57]

Ultimately, therefore, for Miranda, we need to free ourselves from the false ways of thinking that we have acquired in Western society. Hence, the bulk of his work is an examination of Scripture, intended to offer "the 'way of thinking' proper to the Bible."[58] Liberation theology seeks a genuinely biblical justice. As Gutierrez puts it, "justice and right cannot be emptied of the content bestowed on them by the Bible."[59] However, this genuinely biblical justice will not be simply a new set of rules for distribution. Rather, it will be new ways of understanding the meaning of justice.[60] Understood from the praxis of those struggling for justice and liberation, new meanings emerge from Scripture.

Miranda isolates three central messages of Scripture. First, one can know God only through effecting justice. Using established techniques of scriptural exegesis, Miranda argues, for example, that the prohibition against making "graven images" of God arises from the conviction that God cannot be separated from the hearing of God's commands. There is no "God" apart from God's injunctions. Thus, there is no way to "image" God or to know or to speak about God apart from God's commands. God is known only in the response to God's commands.

These commands are commands of justice. Hence, there is no knowledge of God apart from involvement in acts of justice. "To do justice" is used synonymously in Scripture with "to know God."[61] Thus, liberation theology presents a fundamental epistemological challenge: How is God known? The liberationist answers: not through propositions or deductions or theories, but only in the act of doing justice. As Dussel puts it, "theology does not demonstrate from axioms but from the poor."[62]

Second, the biblical God is a God of liberation: "In the view of the Bible, Yahweh is the God who breaks into human history to liberate the oppressed."[63] Miranda points out that in the "P" or priestly strand of the Hebrew Scriptures, God's name is given at the moment of liberation.[64] Indeed, the term *justice* is used interchangeably with the term for God, *Yahweh* (e.g., Jer. 23:6, "Yahweh our justice").[65] In the "J" or Yahwist strand, God is the one who hears the cries of the oppressed.[66] Thus, as Boesak puts it, "the all-surpassing characteristic of Yahweh is his acts in history as the God of justice and liberation for the sake of those who are weak and oppressed."[67]

Two terms are used for justice in the Hebrew Scriptures: *ṣedaqah* and *mishpat*. For Miranda, the term *mishpat* is central. He points out that it is the root both of the laws (*mishpatim*) and also of the word usually translated "judgment." Hence, the meaning of the "last judgment" as well as the discrimination of the true laws of Israel will depend on the meaning of *mishpat*. Linguistic and exegetical study suggests that *mishpat* means eliminating injuries based on injustice.[68] Careful examination of its use in the Hebrew Scriptures suggests that "*mishpat* consists in doing justice to the poor, neither more nor less."[69]

Hence, biblical justice means justice for the poor. Jesus follows this tradition by proclaiming *mishpat* (Matt. 12:18,20).[70] As Gutierrez affirms, "The work of Christ is present simultaneously as a liberation from sin and from all its consequences: despoliation, injustice, hatred."[71] Salvation cannot be separated from social justice. According to Miranda, Paul continues this emphasis on social sin and salvation.[72]

"Justice" is what God does. But what God does is to liberate and love the poor. From the Exodus event to the Beatitudes, God is liberator of the poor. "For the Bible, the root of behavior that can be called 'just' is in the historical fact that constitutes a resume of its faith: God delivered us from Egypt."[73] Jesus is God become poor: born into poverty, living with the poor, addressing "good news" to the poor, lashing out against the rich, and being "poor" or humble in spirit.[74] Jesus' gospel, e.g., the beatitude "blessed are the poor," tells us that God loves the poor, not because they are good, but simply because they are poor.[75]

The poor, therefore, become the litmus test for justice: "To deal with a poor man or woman as Yahweh dealt with his people—this is what it is to be just."[76] This statement must not be misunderstood. In spite of its affinity with Marxist analytic methods and social goals, the view of justice provided in liberation theology is not simply a new version of "to each according to need." Justice is not a simple formula for distribution. Justice would not be accomplished merely by offering programs that meet basic needs of the poor. Justice requires the kind of liberating activity that characterizes God's behavior toward the poor and oppressed.[77]

This sets up the third central affirmation of the liberation approach to justice: there is no separation of "love" and "justice." God's justice is God's love or compassion on those who suffer.[78] God's love is God's justice or liberation of the oppressed.[79] As Boesak maintains, there is no reconciliation without liberation, no loving harmony not based on justice.[80] At the same time, as Dussel maintains, there can be no justice without love. True justice means giving what is due to the other as a *person*, not merely as part of *system*, and this requires love.[81] Hence, differentiating justice and love is "one of the most disastrous errors in the history of Christianity," argues Miranda.[82]

The gospel attacks the roots of all injustice—all breach of love, or sin, and all the "consequences and expressions" of this cleavage in friendship.[83] Gutierrez therefore claims that liberating activity has a threefold dimension: (1) economic, political, and social justice; (2) the emergence of a "new person" in a "new society"; and (3) liberation from sin or selfishness.[84]

Thus, although the capitalist system is seen as unjust by its very nature, socialism or a new economic order is not the sole sum and substance of the "justice" sought by liberation theology. The goals of justice and liberation are "not only to obtain a better standard of living, but also to be able to participate in the socio-economic resources and the decision-making process of the country."[85] Nor is liberation theology concerned merely to support revolution.[86] Understanding of the "totality and complexity" of liberation permits Gutierrez to declare that "the only possible justice is definitive justice."[87]

The justice that is sought by liberation theology is therefore not a formula for distribution. Justice is not a norm or law, but the establishment and maintenance of right relationships or "righteousness."[88] If misery, exploitation, deprivation of basic rights, and lack of respect represent those "grave injustices" that are "rampant" in Latin American society, then "justice" is the opposite. "Justice" would be a condition characterized by adequate structures at all these levels— economic support, political access, and fundamental respect as human beings. As Miranda puts it, "the injustice, the mercilessness, the oppression, and the exploitation to which all cultures have learned to resign themselves are precisely what Yahweh wants to abolish in the world."[89]

Review

Like the bishops and Niebuhr, the liberation approach to justice is grounded in faith. But there are striking differences in the working out of that faith and its implications for justice. For Niebuhr, a biblical view puts stress on the sinfulness of people. For the bishops, a biblical view yields an affirmation of the worth of people and of their interdependence. Miranda would no doubt share these affirmations. But reading Scripture with the eyes of the poor, he finds in it a primary concern for justice focused on God's special love for the poor and oppressed. Justice begins in rejection of injustice. God is a God of justice above all; God is known only in the doing of justice; the doing of justice means doing justice for the poor.

Doing justice for the poor is not, for Miranda, the same as "meeting the needs" of the poor. It is not, as with Rawls, ensuring that the poor benefit from social arrangements that permit others to have more than they do. Nor is it, as with Nozick, ensuring that economic exchanges are fair. Nor is it, as with Niebuhr, ensuring a balance of power. For Miranda, justice for the poor is summed up in God's liberating activity in the Exodus. It is nothing short of liberation of the poor from all forms of oppression. There can be no divisions of economic and political spheres, for justice is all-encompassing.

Critique

Criticisms of liberation theology abound from within and without. There is scarcely an aspect of the "liberation" approach that has not been criticized. Yet, few of these criticisms deal explicitly with the central question of justice. This question is largely ignored or is subsumed under more general criticisms of method, substance, and style. The two most common attacks are those on the scholarship of liberation theology and those on its methodology. Several of these bear at least indirectly on the question of a liberation theory of justice.

Since the liberation approach to justice begins with a reading of the "injustice" of the situation, the reading of the situation is crucial. Critics charge that liberation scholarship is inadequate at this point. Liberation theologians fail to provide the hard data needed to substantiate their interpretations of the situation.[90] They provide little theory regarding how structures work in society and little analysis of power.[91] Their "liberation" paradigm requires acceptance of "dependency" theory, yet they ignore alternate forms of that theory which would yield different readings of the situation.[92] They also ignore the particular oppressions of women.[93]

Most important, some charge that the misery of Latin America is not explained adequately by dependency theory or by the history of capitalist exploitation alone but is due to other factors, such as characteristics of Latin American culture or of human nature. The situation in Latin America (and elsewhere where liberation theology is emerging) may be "unfortunate," critics argue, but this does not make it "unfair."

For instance, Michael Novak charges that U.S. corporations have far too few investments in Latin America to be responsible for the state of Latin American economy.[94] McKenzie charges that Miranda "oversimplifies" the situation, assuming that "a change in the economic and social system will destroy concupiscence."[95] For these critics, the misery of the poor in Latin America is not so much a result of structural injustices as a sign of the sin that affects all people, including the poor.

At this point, criticism of scholarship becomes criticism of theology. The issue is whether liberation theology has too narrow a concept of sin. Wall asserts that "one of the greatest weaknesses in liberation thought is its preoccupation with oppressive systems."[96] This preoccupation leads it to ignore both the phenomenon of individual sin and the tenacity of sin in human life. Thus, liberation theologians fail to be sufficiently self-critical[97] or to recognize that replacing capitalism with socialism will not eradicate all the problems of Latin America. Braaten says flatly, "A theology of the cross debunks every ideology that claims that the original sin that infects all humanity will be removed as a result of structural changes in the world wrought by human praxis."[98]

Liberation theologians are also charged with being "utopian."[99] Contemporary Christian realists argue that liberationists expect historical perfection and fail to distinguish partial fulfillments in history from the final liberation of the kingdom.[100] Following Niebuhr's pessimism about historical possibilities, critics charge that liberationists fail to appreciate the relativity of all human schemes.[101]

Ironically, Niebuhr himself might have defended liberation theologians against their "realist" critics. In his firm belief in the necessity for secular concepts of justice, Niebuhr once wrote, "I would prefer to work with the superficial believers in utopia rather than ally myself with a kind of theological profundity which falsifies the immediate situation."[102] He understood well how necessary the struggle for justice is, and he did not perceive that struggle as a denial of other dimensions of sin: "The victim of injustice cannot cease from contending against his oppressors, even if he has a religious sense of the relativity of all social positions and a contrite recognition of the sin in his own heart."[103]

Theological differences related to understanding the person as a creature before God are based in part on different understandings of

Scripture. Hence, it is to be expected that the scriptural scholarship of liberation theologians has also come under attack.

Critics charge that the liberation reading of Scripture is highly selective.[104] Some argue that it is conservative and ignores important contributions or methods of contemporary biblical scholarship.[105] Hebblethwaite notes, for example, that Miranda ironically does not make use of Marxist modes of analysis of Scripture, e.g., emerging analyses of the socioeconomic base for production of particular biblical texts.[106] McCann argues that when liberation theologians claim to find grounds for contemporary political activity in an interpretation of what God did for the ancient Israelites they assume a kind of analogy between the current and ancient situations that simply does not hold.[107]

Even "friendly critics" such as Sölle and Brueggemann express concern about aspects of Miranda's interpretation of Scripture.[108] Miranda's method involves tracing the appearance of ṣedaqah, mishpat, and other cognate terms related to the theme of justice. Such a thematic approach is not necessarily the best way to address justice in a narrative tradition.[109] For example, when King David had unjustly killed Uriah and taken Bathsheba, the prophet Nathan confronted him with a small parable about a rich man stealing the ewe lamb of a poor man. The terms ṣedaqah and mishpat do not appear in the story, but it is nonetheless an important story about justice from a biblical perspective. To the extent that liberation views are based on scriptural exegesis, the adequacy of that exegesis is central.

Of course, liberationists' reading of Scripture is based on the underlying methodology of praxis—critical reflection arising out of involvement. The real issue is not simply exegesis of texts, but hermeneutics. What are the proper tools for interpretation of both situation and Scripture?

Methods of scriptural interpretation therefore become a "catch–22." On the one hand, using traditional methods of analysis (as Miranda does) in order to mount convincing arguments to scholars in the field exposes liberationists to the charge that they represent a Western-trained "elite" who cannot truly speak for the people of Latin America: "radical Christians of the Third World are not the wretched of the earth, but members of the bourgeois elite."[110] On the other hand, if liberationists eschew established modes of scholarship in order to speak directly for the people, they are attacked for being too simplistic and not maintaining "the minimum of critical sense that one has a right to expect of any rigorous theology today." [111]

The theory of justice proposed by liberation theology arises not simply from Scripture but from the combination of Scripture and praxis. It is the experience of the people that provides the grounds for ethical judgments regarding the demands of justice. Of all the possible challenges to liberation theology, the most vehement are those related to the use of praxis as a method.

The use of this method seems to make experience or history normative. [112] Such a move raises numerous criticisms, from the charge that experience is an inadequate normative base to the charge that it undermines any possibility for a normative base.

Braaten charges that praxis is not complete as a method. Since the historical situation is not characterized by liberation, it is clear that an examination of history or experience alone does not yield the value of liberation. To know that "liberation" is the goal of history is already to presuppose some values that depend on symbols or mythology outside of history. Praxis is therefore not the first step, as claimed, but a second step which is itself dependent on prior theological affirmations. [113] For Braaten and others, praxis is not an adequate normative base; liberation theology must presuppose some view of God which is normative before praxis begins.

Other critics, however, do see liberation theology as depending on praxis. But it is precisely this dependence that presents problems. Norman argues that in using praxis, liberation theologians import Marxist and humanist values under the guise of Christianity. Belief in social change is not a distinctively Christian view, he argues, but rather a modern, liberal view. [114] Braaten agrees with the charge that praxis implies non-Christian values: he calls praxis "the Trojan horse of liberation theology." [115]

Fierro contends that not only are other values slipped in through the concept of praxis, but that ultimately faith is squeezed out: "the social, economic, and political analysis undertaken in the framework of Marxist theory tends to rule out faith in Christ." [116] If the "pulse of history" or the goal of human existence is found in the struggles of the masses, why is any recourse to the gospel necessary? [117] Taking praxis seriously as a method implies ultimately a protean concept of human beings in which all limits disappear. Under such an approach, any notion of a creator God who sets limits to human endeavors or whose actions are needed to complete historical justice ultimately collapses.[118] Thus, while Braaten thinks a view of God is presupposed as a normative base, others think a view of God is excluded as a normative base.

Critics charge that the use of praxis ultimately undermines any possibility for a truly normative perspective. Norman suggests that liberation theology contradicts itself: in order to see Christ's teachings expressed in secular liberation movements, it is necessary to presuppose a clear and agreed understanding of Christ's teachings; yet this is precisely what liberationists refuse to do, since they want to reconstruct the way we understand the scriptural message. If that reconstruction itself depends on the secular movements of the day, then any external "Christian" perspective is lost. Hence he asserts that "they do not have another world to stand upon in order that they may move this one."[119] To fail to recognize that there are values "outside" the liberation movement is to give up the possibility of any perspective on history or any normative stance with regard to history. Liberationists end up with no method of ascertaining that some historical situations are right and others wrong.[120]

Critics also charge that failure to provide an adequate foundation for a normative perspective puts liberation theology on shaky ground when it comes to ethics—and, hence, to a theory of justice. The praxis method, suggests McCann, is antithetical to the doing of ethics. Liberation theology provides a fundamental moral option: solidarity with the oppressed. But the actual requirements of that solidarity can be worked out only by the communities.[121] Thus, the advice given tends to be vague, and liberation theology is limited in its ability to "announce" as well as "denounce."[122] Black liberation theologian James Cone notes that the absence of historical models adequately embodying the liberationist's political and theological imagination makes it difficult "to speak meaningfully about the socialist alternative."[123] In short, there is a lack of clear development of "ethics," understood as a system of imperatives or a normative reference.

Liberation methodology limits its capacity to make definitive judgments about justice, since it eschews principles in favor of the historical experience of the community. While Gutierrez declares that Scripture tells us that the only justice is "definitive" justice, some critics would charge that his basic method makes such an appeal to Scripture unacceptable and thus undermines his concept of "definitive justice." Miranda appeals to Marxist theory on the one hand and Scripture on the other as grounds for a theory of justice. To many critics, the juxtaposition of Marxism and Scripture is self-defeating and contradictory. Hence, Fierro charges that liberation theology—at least in its Latin American version—remains largely "rhetorical" and is not capable of being a "truly significant theology with claims to validity" for the contemporary world.[124]

Assessment

Yet, none of these critics challenges directly the central liberation claims that the Judeo-Christian God is a God of justice, that to know God is to do justice, or that justice and love cannot be separated. As Gutierrez puts it, those who accuse liberation theology of being a "bastard mixture" of theology, sociology, and politics, nonetheless "do not undertake to disagree with the content of our reflection."[125]

Critics may challenge liberation theology for failing to focus on individual sin, but few would deny the importance of structural sin. Only a few would go so far as to say that the situation in Latin America or South Africa, or other places where liberation theology is emerging, is not indeed characterized by injustice. And, while they might wish a more detailed mapping of that injustice and a more "principled" approach to understanding what justice would mean by contrast, the force of liberation theology is being everywhere felt.

Indeed, some who would criticize liberation theology on the theoretical level nonetheless find liberation theologians to be right in practice. As Hunsinger suggests, the sheer volume of the Bible devoted to hunger, justice, and the poor gives credence to the central concerns of liberation theology.[126] Moreover, both Weir and Brueggemann suggest that liberation theology makes an important contribution to questions of hermeneutics by focusing attention on what happens to the interpretation of Scripture when it is viewed "from the underside."[127]

But perhaps it is the very breadth and indeterminateness of the liberation understanding of justice that is its greatest contribution. Emil Brunner once noted that the scope of "justice" in the Bible is immense, but that the breadth of meaning of the term has been restricted in the modern age. Whereas justice originally meant "righteousness," it has come to mean "giving to each what is due."[128] Under the influence of philosophy, theologians narrowed their use of the term.

This is precisely what liberationists have thus far refused to do. Justice is nothing less than "right relationship" and encompasses every aspect of human living. Liberation theology does not give us a tight philosophical theory of justice. But it gives a sense of the fullness of justice—of the intrusion of justice into every arena of human life. Above all, it gives us the sense of a justice known primarily through the experience of injustice.

Conclusion

So where have we come with our explorations of the elephant? What are the gifts and legacies of each approach? What are the possibilities for a theory of justice? Let us begin with a quick review.

Six Fragments on Justice

From Mill and the utilitarians, we get a vision of a good that transcends and yet incorporates individual rights. Claims are accepted as the core of justice, but claims are always derived from and dependent on the maximizing of utility. To be sure, justice for Mill includes a fundamental sense of equality, since each person's good is to count as much as each other's. Yet there is no standard of equality as the goal or pattern of distribution. Instead, the possibilities of the greater good overall present the challenge that all subsequent theories of justice must encounter.

It is this challenge to which Rawls responds. Rawls, too, acknowledges the possibility of inequality in distribution for the sake of a greater gain. However, not just any gain will do: it matters who receives the benefits and who bears the burdens. Whereas utilitarians would have us picture society as an individual "writ large," making choices about gains and losses, for Rawls the gains to some do not compensate for losses to others. The vision of a common good is not alone sufficient, and must be tempered by a distributive principle that benefits the least advantaged. In Rawls' own view, the theory ultimately works toward an equality of distribution, though it does not require equality as its distributive principle.

Nozick wants to begin from the same Kantian principles as Rawls, respecting the rights and reason of individuals. But he rejects utterly any substantive equalitarianism as the requirement of justice. Rather, justice becomes the product of free choice and exchange. To set any requirements for equality of distribution is to violate human freedom. It is therefore freedom, not equality, that constitutes the core of justice. This is the insurmountable challenge that Nozick raises: is freedom to be sacrificed in the interests of equality?

Neither do the bishops call for substantive equality. Yet, they reject any simple notion that free choice alone—especially in the market system—yields justice. Drawing on a long Catholic tradition, they propose three principles of justice: commutative fairness in exchange, distributive attention to need, and, perhaps most important, social requirements for participation. Theirs is a vision of justice based on the notion that human dignity is achieved only in community and that the resources of the earth "belong" ultimately only to God.

Niebuhr adds to this synthetic picture the discordant note of sin. Individual rights and group interests are not so easily compatible with the "greater good" or with the "common good" as Mill, on the one hand, and Catholic tradition, on the other, might have it. Justice is not the result of philosophical theory, for reasoning and theory themselves become suspect. Justice in the "real" world is a constant process of compromise with the realities of sin and injustice. Niebuhr leaves us distressingly without clear rules for justice, though equality emerges as both a procedural and a substantive principle. What he does leave us with is a sense of the necessity for historical compromise and hence of the inadequacies of every concrete achievement of justice.

Miranda and other liberation theologians accept and advance Niebuhr's focus on sin. Justice begins, not with theory, but with the concrete realities of injustice experienced by the oppressed and illumined by the God of the Bible. Niebuhr's distrust of reason is carried to its full implications of the "epistemological privilege" of the poor: only those who suffer injustice and are involved in the struggle for justice can know what justice is. Justice has become not merely structural, but systemic.

Of Elephants and Justice

Here, in brief, are six fragments of justice—six descriptions of the elephant. What, then, is the nature of the beast? These theories can be assessed from the perspective of substance and of method. Let us begin with substance.

Tradition has it that the formal principle of distributive justice is "to each what is due."[1] In one way or another, most of the authors considered here would accept that formula, at least to a point. But when it comes to deciding what is "due," they would give the formal statement of justice radically different content. If justice is "to each according to. . .," then our six theories might look like this:

- *Mill:* to each according to those tendencies of actions that maximize overall utility;
- *Rawls:* to each according to a basic structure that benefits the least advantaged (within limits set by equal political rights, equal opportunity, and just savings for future generations);
- *Nozick:* to each according to the choices that have given them entitlements;
- *Bishops:* to each according to their dignity as creatures made in the image of God (with duties and rights consonant with that image, and spelled out in a threefold notion of justice);
- *Niebuhr:* to each according to principles of freedom, and especially of equality, tempered by love or equity;
- *Miranda:* to each according to God's interventions in history to liberate the poor and oppressed.

The differences are striking. Does justice require maximizing utility, benefiting the least advantaged, accepting the consequences of choice, honoring human dignity, treating equally, or liberating the poor and oppressed? Striking, too, is the absence of some traditional notions such as the Aristotelian claim that justice means distribution in accord with merit.

The differences are just as striking if we turn from substance to method. How are we to arrive at a theory of justice? Here, our authors might complete the sentence, "the requirements of justice are derived by. . ." as follows:

- *Mill:* the requirements of justice are derived by looking for the common core in accepted notions of what is just and unjust;
- *Rawls:* the requirements of justice are derived by rational choice in a "fair" setting;
- *Nozick:* the requirements of justice are those minimal rights derived by deduction from the Kantian maxim to treat each person as an end and not merely as a means;
- *Bishops:* the requirements of justice are derived by embodying a faith-based vision of justice in traditional philosophical and theological principles of duties and rights;
- *Niebuhr:* the requirements of justice are derived by the faith-based principle of love compromising with the realities of sin;
- *Miranda:* the requirements of justice are derived by biblical confirmation of Marxist analysis of injustices experienced by the oppressed.

Again, the differences are striking. Are the requirements of justice derived by observations of the elite, by reason abstracted from history, by deduction, by reason complementing revelation, by faith compromising with history, or by biblical and Marxist analysis? Not only have those examining the elephant come to different conclusions about the nature of the beast named "justice," but they use such different tools for their examination that it is only to be expected that sometimes they appear to be describing different beasts altogether.

These characterizations of our six blindfolded explorers are gross oversimplifications, bordering on, if not slipping into, caricature. Yet if there is any truth in these characterizations, they suggest a serious problem for all those interested in this elephant. As stated, they imply that there is no common ground for a theory of justice. Neither in method nor in substance is there sufficient agreement to think that even within our limited historical context we can have a theory of justice. As MacIntyre suggests, we do appear to be left with moral fragments that no longer have and are incapable of having a common ground or supporting base.

Perhaps this is due in part to the different concerns of our theorists. Rawls' attention is directed to the basic structure of society, while Niebuhr's was directed toward a fundamental view of human nature.

Nozick's attention is directed to the necessities and limits of the state, while Miranda's is focused on biblical ways of thinking. Mill's attention was focused on criteria for right action in general, while the bishops focus more directly on poverty in the United States. Different starting places yield different fragments on justice.

Of Blindfolded Exploration

The differences do not divide neatly along philosophical and theological lines. In some ways, there is as much difference between Rawls and Nozick as between Rawls and the National Conference of Catholic Bishops. Both the bishops and Niebuhr could be and have been accused of adopting many of the "liberal" presuppositions that permeate the philosophical theories considered here. Thus, in spite of striking differences, there are also striking similarities.

Yet, at one point, which is worth considering, there does seem to be a division along the line of philosophy versus theology. It is the point of assessment of fundamental assumptions of the capitalist market and private property system.

All three philosophical systems considered here represent support for and affirmation of a market-based, capitalist economic system. With its reliance on the "greatest net good," utilitarianism became the base for much economic theory that supports capitalism. Problems experienced by workers in such a system are not easily recognized by a theory in which gains to some can outweigh losses to others. As long as the overall economic system is thought to work for the "greater good" in the long run, losses to the poor in the short run are deemed a "necessary trade-off" that does not make a system unjust. This is seen very clearly in some of the responses from the business community to the bishops' letter.

Rawls, too, appears to defend democratic capitalism. Although he argues that his principles of justice are compatible with both capitalist and socialist economic systems, basic acceptance of capitalism is assured. So long as the least advantaged are thought to "benefit" from the market system, no injustice has been done. On what is dubbed the "trickle down" theory, benefits to those at the top in a capitalist economy are always thought to "trickle down" to some benefits for those at the bottom. By Rawls' theory, this makes capitalism basically a just economy.

Nozick gives the most explicit support for a capitalist market exchange system based on the right of private property. Indeed, he indicates that he believes contemporary capitalist societies do not violate the principles of justice in exchange that he offers. Whatever distribution of goods occurs within an economy is just, so long as it is the consequence of proper market exchanges. There is no sense of any limits necessary to protect the poor.

Thus, although the utilitarians, Rawls, and Nozick hold very different basic theories of justice, in practice they all support forms of capitalist "free market" exchange and private property.

The picture changes quickly when we turn to the theological theories. None of them gives such unqualified support to capitalism or to private property.

Though the Catholic tradition continues to support the right of private ownership, that right has always been subject to the constraints of the common good on the use of property. Writing within the North American context, the bishops do not address strongly the growing tendency in Catholic social teaching to support expropriation of lands. Nor do they offer a fundamental criticism of capitalism. Yet their support is clearly qualified, and they raise grave concerns about the impact of ·capitalism on the poor.

Niebuhr in his early years adopted explicitly Marxist critiques of capitalism. To be sure, he was also critical of socialist alternatives. Nonetheless, it is clear that a "free exchange" system based on private property would not for him represent economic justice. It gives too much power to those in control of capital, and, for Niebuhr, justice always required a balancing of such power.

Miranda is one of the liberation theologians most outspokenly opposed to capitalism. For him, the capitalist system that permits "differentiating" ownership and the development of classes is intrinsically evil. Justice is antithetical to any system that permits the poor to suffer so.

Once again, although all three Christian perspectives offer quite different approaches to, and theories of, justice, in practice they appear to agree at least on the question of capitalism.

Thus, it seems that a clear line can be drawn at least on this one issue, if not on others. Even here, however, I venture to suggest that those who describe the elephant so differently nonetheless may profit from dialog with each other.

Surely the most radically different approaches are those of Nozick and Miranda. They seem to be at opposite ends of the economic—and possibly the political—spectrum. As different and irreconcilable as their views appear, however, there are some interesting common grounds.

Liberation theology arises out of historical injustices. But what is the nature of these injustices? Miranda suggests that the micro-level injustices of wage contracts can be used to develop a macro-level analogy: the poor would not have agreed to the system that puts them in their current poverty. These claims make sense if one assumes a base akin to Nozick's theory of commutative justice. If the original acquisition is fair, and if the exchange is fair, then the resulting division is fair. Surely the liberation charge is either that the original acquisition was not fair (e.g., lands and goods were stolen rather than purchased) or that the exchange was not fair (coercion was involved, grounds for setting a fair price were not mutually agreed).

Miranda acknowledges this when he says that "commutative justice itself carries within it the whole problem of distribution."[2] Thus, in order for the charges of "injustice" leveled by liberation theology to be established, there must be some theory about right exchange and fairness in choice. Nozick's theory might provide some base for liberation accusations. In this sense, the liberation perspective needs Nozick.

But Nozick also needs the liberation perspective. Nozick claims to establish a historical approach to justice. But he provides no mechanisms by which that approach can be tested. His conclusion that capitalism meets the demands of justice rests on speculation, not evidence. Liberation theology provides the historical experiences necessary to test the truth of Nozick's claim. If liberation theology needs Nozick to demonstrate why the situation in Latin America is genuinely "unfair" and not just "unfortunate," Nozick needs liberation theology to put flesh on the bones of his historical approach to justice.

But then if it turns out that liberation theology is correct, and that the world situation is characterized largely by injustice, something else will be needed. Nozick nods toward the necessity for a theory of rectification of injustice, but fails to develop that theory. Yet, it is precisely this that may be the most important clue toward establishing distributive justice in our age.

If injustice is the beginning point, then we may need different theories of justice. In rejecting the classical distinction of distributive, retributive, and commutative justice, Feinberg suggests that "an equally useful" way of classifying the data of justice and one which promises "more rewarding theoretical insights" is a classification according to types of injustice.[3] Perhaps another perspective for exploring the elephant is needed. A theory of justice is needed that is truly historical and that takes seriously the problem of rectification of injustice. If *mishpat* is to be the measure, then *ṣedaqah* must be the plumb line. It is toward that plumb line that my next volume will move.

Notes

Introduction

1. Alasdair MacIntyre, *After Virtue* (Notre Dame: University of Notre Dame Press, 1981), p. 104.
2. Joel Feinberg has proposed that traditional classifications of justice—distributive, retributive, and commutative—are not particularly helpful. See "Noncomparative Justice," in J. Feinberg and Hyman Gross, *Justice: Selected Readings* (Belmont, Calif.: Wadsworth, 1977), p. 55. His proposal reflects the ambiguities to be encountered in this volume.
3. Explicitly excluded from our study is the arena of retributive justice. Yet, even here, John Stuart Mill does not separate the distributive from the retributive aspects of justice.
4. Another tempting alternative is Emil Brunner's *Justice and the Social Order* (London: Lutterworth, 1945), which presents a more classic two-kingdoms approach than does Niebuhr. The choice of Niebuhr instead of Brunner is justified by Niebuhr's importance to the formation of Protestant thought in the United States.
5. See Paul Ramsey, "Love and Law," in *Reinhold Niebuhr: His Religious, Social, and Political Thought,* ed. C. W. Kegley and R. W. Bretall (New York: Macmillan, 1956), p. 95. I concur with John Bennett's claims that the essential structure of Niebuhr's thought was formed in the 1930s and 1940s; that period, therefore, represents Niebuhr's thought here. See John C. Bennett, "Reinhold Niebuhr's Social Ethics," in Kegley and Bretall, p. 47.
6. Reinhold Niebuhr, "Reply to Interpretation and Criticism," ibid., p. 434.
7. Liberation theology is often the result of groups of people working together for liberation. Thus, as Gustavo Gutierrez puts it, "it makes little difference whose name appears on articles and books." See *The Power of the Poor in History* (Maryknoll, N.Y.: Orbis, 1983), p. 204.
8. Liberation theology is emerging in Asia, Africa, and North America as well as in Latin America. Obviously, the liberation concerns of a Korean farmer will

not be the same as those of a black industrial worker in North America. Women add some distinctive concerns as well. I regret that none of the six theories represented here is a feminist theory. I chose Latin American liberation theology, not out of a conviction that it is the only, nor even the most important context for liberation theology, but out of appreciation for Miranda's contributions to an understanding of justice.

9. This does not mean, however, that no women are represented here. John Stuart Mill often attributed his inspiration to his wife. Much contemporary liberation theology is done by women.

Chapter 1. The Utilitarian Challenge: John Stuart Mill

1. J. J. C. Smart, "Extreme and Restricted Utilitarianism," in *Contemporary Utilitarianism*, ed. Michael D. Bayles (New York: Doubleday, 1968), pp. 99-141.
2. Richard B. Brandt, "Toward a Credible Form of Utilitarianism," in ibid., pp. 143-186.
3. Nicholas Rescher, *Distributive Justice: A Constructive Critique of the Utilitarian Theory of Distribution* (Indianapolis: Bobbs-Merrill, 1966), p. x.
4. John Stuart Mill, *Utilitarianism* (New York: Bobbs-Merrill, 1957).
5. Ibid., p. 10.
6. For Jeremy Bentham's argument, see *An Introduction to the Principles of Morals and Legislation*, ed. J. H. Burns and H. L. A. Hart (London: Methuen, 1982), pp. 11-12.
7. Ibid., p. 13.
8. Mill, *Utilitarianism*, pp. 7 and 48. However, Henry Sidgwick later argued that this is not a "proof" of utilitarianism; he drew his defense of the theory largely on the basis of its coherence with and ability to systematize the maxims of "common sense." See *The Methods of Ethics* (London: Macmillan, 1962), pp. 419f.
9. Mill, *Utilitarianism*, p. 12.
10. See David Lyons, *Forms and Limits of Utilitarianism* (Oxford: Clarendon, 1965), p. 9. W. D. Ross in *The Right and the Good* (Oxford: Clarendon, 1930), p. 17, argues that "ideal" utilitarianism is logically the more basic of the two.
11. Teleology is contrasted with deontology, in which the right is prior to the good. The theory of John Rawls, to be considered in the next chapter, is a form of deontology.
12. Bentham, *An Introduction*, pp. 39-40.
13. See J. J. C. Smart, "Extreme and Restricted Utilitarianism."
14. Bentham, *An Introduction*, p. 40.
15. Mill, *Utilitarianism*, pp. 30-31.
16. Mill, *Utilitarianism*, p. 31.
17. J. O. Urmson, "The Interpretation of the Moral Philosophy of J. S. Mill," in *Contemporary Utilitarianism*.
18. H. J. McCloskey, "A Non-Utilitarian Approach to Punishment," in *Contemporary Utilitarianism*, pp. 239-259, argues that the act-utilitarian is committed to such a position. However, T. L. S. Sprigge, "A Utilitarian Reply to Dr. McCloskey," in *Contemporary Utilitarianism*, pp. 261-269, defends utilitarianism against the charge.

19. Bentham, *An Introduction*, p. 1. While Bentham notes that "the business of government is to promote the happiness of the society, by punishing and rewarding," his exclusive interest in punishment takes him away from the arena of reward, which is more the arena of distributive justice (ibid., p. 74).
20. Mill, *Utilitarianism*, p. 53.
21. Ibid., p. 73.
22. David Hume, "Of Justice" (section 3 of *An Enquiry Concerning the Principles of Morals*, first published in 1751), reprinted in J. Feinberg and H. Gross, *Justice: Selected Readings* (Belmont, Calif: Wadsworth, 1977), p. 75.
23. Ibid., p. 76. Note that Hume deals with justice, not as a set of principles for distribution, but as a *virtue:* "the cautious, jealous virtue of justice" (p. 75).
24. Ibid., p. 77. Sidgwick criticizes Hume at this point, arguing that what Hume calls "justice" is really nothing but "order" (*The Methods of Ethics,* p. 440). Rawls argues that Hume is not a true utilitarian, since what he calls "utility" really amounts to a form of common good rather than a strict utilitarian calculus in which the good of some compensates for losses to others (*A Theory of Justice,* pp. 32-33).
25. Hume, "Of Justice," p. 78, declares that it is "requisite, for the peace and interest of society, that men's possessions should be separated." Elsewhere he speaks of establishing rules for property "which are, on the whole, most *useful* and *beneficial*" (ibid., p. 79).
26. Ibid., pp. 81-82.
27. Mill, *Utilitarianism*, p. 78.
28. Ibid., pp. 54-57.
29. Ibid., p. 60.
30. Ibid., p. 62.
31. Ibid., p. 65. It is interesting to note here that Sidgwick takes almost exactly the opposite approach. He suggests that justice arises from the "natural impulse to requite benefits," focusing on reward instead of punishment or vengeance as the foundation of justice. Indeed, Sidgwick's approach leads him to suggest that the real foundation for justice is gratitude. See *The Methods of Ethics,* Book 3, Chap. 5: "Justice" (New York: Dover, 1966), p. 279.
32. Mill, *Utilitarianism*, p. 67.
33. Ibid., p. 74.
34. Ibid., p. 76.
35. Ibid., p. 72. Mill does not show *how* the utilitarian formula helps to solve the problem any better than the various appeals to "justice." He merely *asserts* that this is the case.
36. Ibid., p. 73.
37. Among the strongest of those rights for Mill were basic rights of liberty (see *On Liberty*). Clearly, Mill envisioned no basic conflict between the "greatest good" overall and the protection of fundamental liberties, such as freedom of thought.
38. Ibid., p. 57.
39. W. D. Ross, *The Right and the Good*, Chap. 2.
40. Ibid., p. 38.
41. John Rawls, *A Theory of Justice* (Cambridge, Mass.: Harvard University Press, 1971), p. 15; see also p. 65 and p. 4: "justice denies that loss of freedom for some is made right by a greater good shared by others."

42. Ibid., p. 27.
43. Ross, *The Right and the Good*, p. 22.
44. Richard B. Brandt, "Toward a Credible Form of Utilitarianism," p. 147. J. J. C. Smart, "Extreme and Restricted Utilitarianism," p. 111, following Sidgwick, might argue in response that such acts are indeed *right* though they are to be *condemned:* "a right action may be rationally condemned."
45. Alan Donagan, "Is There a Credible Form of Utilitarianism?" in *Contemporary Utilitarianism*, p. 198. Lyons makes the same point in more subdued manner: "no pure utilitarian theory can account for some of our strongest convictions" (*Forms and Limits*, p. XI).
46. Mill, *Utilitarianism*, p. 10; Bentham, *An Introduction*, pp. 11f.
47. John Rawls, "Two Concepts of Rules," in *Contemporary Utilitarianism*, pp. 59-98.
48. Ibid., p. 95.
49. Lyons, however, has argued (*Forms and Limits*, p. 193) that promises do not constitute a "practice" in the way Rawls intends.
50. Ibid., pp. 184-186.
51. Brandt, "Toward a Credible Form of Utilitarianism," pp. 164-165, argues that rules must be learnable.
52. As J. J. C. Smart puts it ("Extreme and Restricted Utilitarianism," p. 115), "if 'act optimifically' is itself one of our rules then there will always be a conflict of rules whenever to keep a rule is not itself optimific. If this is so, restricted utilitarianism collapses into extreme utilitarianism." While Smart here argues for the priority of extreme or act-utilitarianism because of this "collapse," others have seen the collapse as a fault of rule-utilitarianism that renders it no better than act-utilitarianism. See, for example, H. J. McCloskey, "An Examination of Restricted Utilitarianism," in *Contemporary Utilitarianism*, pp. 124-127; see also Lyons, *Forms and Limits*.
53. H. J. McCloskey, "A Non-Utilitarian Approach to Punishment," in *Contemporary Utilitarianism*, p. 253.
54. Donagan, "Is There a Credible Form of Utilitarianism?" pp. 194-195.
55. Sidgwick, *The Methods of Ethics*, p. 492, appears to acknowledge this. He suggests, however, that it is "practically expedient" to retain the distinction.
56. Mill, *Utilitarianism*, pp. 15f.
57. Ibid., p. 22.
58. Ibid., p. 76.
59. Cf. Rescher, *Distributive Justice*, p. 25.
60. Cf. Sidgwick, *The Methods of Ethics*, p. 415.
61. Rescher, *Distributive Justice*, p. 27.
62. See the discussion in Rawls, *A Theory of Justice*, pp. 161f.
63. Rescher, *Distributive Justice*, p. 29.
64. Cf. ibid., p. 31. Rescher proposes as an equity principle a rule of "least square deviation from the average" (p. 32).
65. Ibid., p. 48.
66. Ibid., p. 56.
67. Ross, *The Right and the Good*, p. 35.
68. Rescher, *Distributive Justice*, p. 54.
69. Ibid., pp. 82 and 63.

70. According to A. D. Woozley, for example, A. M. Honore includes in the list of claims the concept of "special relations" which does not appear on Rescher's list and which Woozley himself is disinclined to accept; see Woozley, "Injustice," in *Studies in Ethics,* American Philosophical Quarterly Monograph Series 7 (1973).

71. Rescher, *Distributive Justice,* p. 73.

72. This is in fact the argument that Sidgwick makes. The breaking of a promise, he suggests, disappoints deeply held expectations, which is an evil (*The Methods of Ethics,* p. 443). Sidgwick also explicitly acknowledges a notion of justice as reward for merit; the requital of desert, he suggests, "constitutes the chief element of Ideal Justice. . ." (p. 283).

73. Lyons (*Forms and Limits,* p. 172) argues, for example, that the utilitarian might wish to support justice by arguing that the one who does not contribute to an enterprise and nonetheless wishes to benefit from that enterprise "sets a bad example." But then the utilitarian has presupposed that it is "wrong" to benefit without contributing. That is, some notion of justice is there prior to the utilitarian calculus.

74. Cf. Ross, *The Right and the Good,* p. 23; Rawls, *A Theory of Justice,* p. 91.

75. Rescher, *Distributive Justice,* p. 10.

76. Sidgwick, *The Methods of Ethics,* p. 436.

77. Lyons, *Forms and Limits,* p. 162. Note that Lyons suggests that fairness can be a prerequisite for achieving utility, e.g., in order to obtain a full house, extra theater seats must be divided; a fair division will ensure use of the seats (pp. 169-170).

78. Richard B. Brandt, *Ethical Theory* (Englewood Cliffs, N.J.: Prentice-Hall, 1959), p. 425.

79. Mill, *Utilitarianism,* pp. 77-78.

80. Brandt, *Ethical Theory,* p. 422.

81. In a fascinating essay, Joel Feinberg discusses the justice of judgments. Untrue assessments of one's merits and demerits is, according to Feinberg, a primary instance of injustice. I shall attempt here to be as "fair" as possible to those approaches and theories under consideration! See Joel Feinberg, "Noncomparative Justice," in J. Feinberg and H. Gross, *Justice: Selected Readings.*

82. Rescher, *Distributive Justice,* p. 92.

83. Indeed, Rescher (ibid., pp. 106-107) proposes that the rules of distributive justice may differ depending on the type of economy. In an economy of scarcity (e.g., where there is not enough to provide a minimal level for all), seeming inequities may be optimal (so that some, at least, survive); in an economy of sufficiency, equity and distribution in accord with claims would be the just approach; in an economy of abundance, some inequities may "pay for themselves" by increasing the goods available for distribution and serving justice in the larger sense.

84. Brandt, *Ethical Theory,* pp. 430-431.

85. Rescher, *Distributive Justice,* p. 102.

Chapter 2. A Contract Response: John Rawls

1. Robert Paul Wolff, *Understanding Rawls: A Reconstruction and Critique of* A Theory of Justice (Princeton: Princeton University Press, 1977), p. 11.

2. John Rawls, *A Theory of Justice* (Cambridge, Mass.: Harvard University Press, 1971). Rawls intends to provide an alternative to the two major theories that dominated the early part of this century: utilitarianism, on the one hand, and deontological intuitive theories, on the other. However, it is clear that utilitarianism sets the major agenda for his work.

3. Ibid., p. 11.

4. Rawls (ibid., p. 7) notes that basic structures in society always favor some starting positions, and thus incorporate inequalities. His overriding concern is to "look for a conception of justice that nullifies the accidents of natural endowment and the contingencies of social circumstance" (p. 15).

5. Ibid., p. 12.

6. Ibid.

7. Ibid., p. 516.

8. Ibid., pp. 136f.

9. Ibid., p. 137.

10. Ibid., pp. 126-127.

11. Ibid., p. 128.

12. Ibid., pp. 137f.

13. Ibid., p. 176.

14. Ibid., pp. 144f.

15. Ibid., p. 143.

16. Ibid., pp. 143, 148-149. *Envy* is used here in a somewhat technical sense, in which it can be distinguished from jealousy. Robert Nozick, *Anarchy, State, and Utopia* (New York: Basic Books, 1974), p. 239, proposes that the envious person prefers that neither have a good, rather than that the other have it while she or he does not.

17. Rawls, *A Theory of Justice,* p. 8. Rawls notes explicitly that he is looking for an "ideal" situation of justice because the "nature and aims of a perfectly just society is the fundamental part of the theory of justice" (p. 9). Taking this "ideal" approach has the advantage of avoiding questions about compensatory or reparative justice.

18. Ibid., p. 302.

19. Ibid. Rawls distinguishes two circumstances under which liberty might be limited. A less extensive liberty for all is sometimes permissible in the interest of strengthening the total system of liberty. A less than equal liberty must be acceptable to those with the lesser liberty, presumably because it strengthens their future liberties. Rawls does acknowledge that under circumstances of extreme duress, there may be times when people would prefer greater economic gains to liberty; however, these are only for situations of dire stress (p. 542).

20. This is indeed what Rawls suggests they would initially consider (ibid., p. 150).

21. Ibid., p. 539.

22. The figures have been changed here, but I am indebted to Wolff for the basic example (*Understanding Rawls,* pp. 30f.).

23. Cf. Rawls, *A Theory of Justice,* p. 151.

24. "It hardly seems likely that persons who view themselves as equals, entitled to press their claims upon one another, would agree to a principle which may require lesser life prospects for some simply for the sake of a greater sum of advantages enjoyed by others" (ibid., p. 14).

25. Ibid., p. 15.
26. See ibid., pp. 152-156.
27. Benjamin R. Barber, "Justifying Justice: Problems of Psychology, Politics, and Measurement in Rawls," in *Reading Rawls*, ed. Norman Daniels (New York: Basic Books, n.d.), p. 297.
28. Rawls, *A Theory of Justice*, p. 83.
29. Ibid., p. 302.
30. Ibid., p. 62.
31. Social cooperation requires reciprocal advantages, claims Rawls (ibid., p. 33). He suggests that the utilitarian approach requires too much identification with the plight of others (p. 198).
32. A complete theory of justice requires not only principles for institutional arrangements but also for individuals. Here Rawls proposes a principle of fairness that requires that we do what the rules of fair institutions would require and a range of "natural duties" such as nonmaleficence, beneficence, etc. (ibid., pp. 110-117). The important question about relationship between such principles and those for institutions simply cannot be addressed here. At least one critic, William A. Galston, *Justice and the Human Good* (Chicago: University of Chicago Press, 1980), p. 4, argues that political life cannot be separated from "natural" duties.
33. Rawls, *A Theory of Justice*, p. 253. Rawls asserts: "Properly understood, then, the desire to act justly derives in part from the desire to express most fully what we are or can be, namely, free and equal rational beings with a liberty to choose" (p. 256).
34. "Pure" procedural justice is distinguished from "perfect" and "imperfect" procedural justice. In each of the latter cases, there is an independent standard for assessing the justice of the outcome, and the only question is whether the procedures are guaranteed to give that outcome. For example, justice in criminal law requires that only the truly guilty be found guilty; however, the court system does not guarantee that result, so it is an instance of "imperfect" procedural justice. In "pure" procedural justice, there is no such independent standard for determining the justice of the results. Whatever results from the procedure is "just" by definition (ibid., pp. 85-89).
35. Distributive justice, says Rawls, is not the same as "allocative" justice (ibid., p. 88). That is, justice is not determined by looking at some pattern or end-state of goods, but by looking at the procedures involved in the basic structures of society.
36. Ibid., p. 18.
37. Ibid., p. 21.
38. See ibid., pp. 48f.
39. Ibid., p. 20.
40. For example, Rawls proposes a four-stage implementation procedure for the application of principles to the various aspects of political and social life (ibid., part II).
41. Ibid., p. 310.
42. Several volumes are devoted entirely to a critique of Rawls and others take Rawls as the epitome of contemporary liberal theory. For the former, see *Reading Rawls;* R. P. Wolff, *Understanding Rawls;* and Brian Barry, *The Liberal Theory of Justice: A Critical Examination of the Principal Doctrines in* A Theory of Justice

by John Rawls (Oxford: Oxford University Press, 1973). For the latter, see Michael J. Sandel, *Liberalism and the Limits of Justice* (Cambridge: Cambridge University Press, 1982); and George Parkin Grant, *English Speaking Justice* (Notre Dame: Notre Dame University Press, 1985).

43. See Milton Fisk, "History and Reason in Rawls' Moral Theory," and Richard W. Miller, "Rawls and Marxism," both in *Reading Rawls*. Note, however, that there is at least one Marxist defense of Rawls: Jeffrey H. Reiman, "The Labor Theory of the Difference Principle," in *Philosophy and Public Affairs*, vol. 12, no. 2 (Spring, 1983), pp. 133-159.

44. Fisk, "History and Reason," p. 57.

45. Wolff, *Understanding Rawls*, pp. 122-123.

46. Sandel, *Liberalism*, p. 174. Ackerman makes the same criticism, suggesting that Rawls operates on a "false individualism" that fails to acknowledge cultural influences on the self. See Bruce J. Ackerman, *Social Justice in the Liberal State* (New Haven: Yale University Press, 1980), p. 345. Sandel and George Parkin Grant also charge that Rawls' alliance of Kant and contract theory is an uneasy alliance at best. The "circumstances of justice" which Rawls adopts from Hume are empirical judgments. Thus, for Sandel, Rawls cannot claim that justice is the first virtue of social institutions, but only of institutions in those societies that have certain characteristics that fit the Humean empiricist assumptions. Not only may there be other virtues for society, but justice—as a narrow kind of calculation of interests—may even be a vice on occasion. Grant argues that Rawls tries to derive fairness from self-interest, while the "very core of Kant's thought is his sharp division between self-interest and fairness" (*English Speaking Justice,* p. 99).

47. Galston, *Justice and the Human Good,* p. 115.

48. Rawls, *A Theory of Justice,* p. 149.

49. Ibid., pp. 28f.

50. James S. Fishkin, *Justice, Equal Opportunity, and the Family* (New Haven: Yale University Press, 1983), p. 183.

51. Rawls, *A Theory of Justice,* p. 15, explicitly argues that one might reject the method and nonetheless accept the principles of "justice as fairness."

52. H. L. A. Hart, "Rawls on Liberty and Its Priority," in *Reading Rawls*, p. 240.

53. Ibid., p. 245. It is not altogether clear that the "natural duties" of beneficence and non-maleficence will always fill the gap.

54. Brian Barry, *The Liberal Theory of Justice*, p. 117, makes an analogous argument about social goods: though it is true that in general we want more of the basic goods, he suggests that we would not always want more if the price is that others also have more. It may be better to be poor in a poor society than rich in a rich one.

55. Hart, "Rawls on Liberty," p. 248. Hart also questions whether it would be rational for those in the original position to choose such a limiting principle when they are not sure what the circumstances of society will be. If they are not sure what stage their society has reached, why would they choose to limit liberty only for the sake of liberty?

56. Rawls, *A Theory of Justice,* p. 204.

57. Norman Daniels, "Equal Liberty and Unequal Worth of Liberty," in *Reading Rawls*, p. 263.

58. Ibid., p. 256.
59. Barry, *The Liberal Theory*, pp. 52, 60f.
60. Ackerman, *Social Justice*, p. 341.
61. Wolff, *Understanding Rawls*, pp. 134-135; Barber, "Justifying Justice," p. 303; Barry, *The Liberal Theory*, pp. 45-47.
62. Barber, "Justifying Justice," p. 298.
63. Thomas Nagel, "Rawls on Justice," in *Reading Rawls*, p. 12; see also Barry, *The Liberal Theory*, p. 97.
64. R. M. Hare, "Rawls' Theory of Justice," in *Reading Rawls*, p. 104. Others argue that under the conditions of the original position—and possibly even with the maximin strategy—the parties would choose some variant of utilitarianism. That is, for all of Rawls' criticism of utilitarianism, he has not shown that under the ideal conditions of the "well-ordered society" it is any less appealing than his difference principle. See, e.g., David Lyons, "Nature and Soundness of the Contract and Coherence Arguments," in *Reading Rawls*, p. 166.
65. Wolff, *Understanding Rawls*, p. 161. Hare concurs: "The truth is that it is a wide open question how the [people in the original position] would choose" ("Rawls' Theory of Justice," p. 106).
66. Hare, "Rawls' Theory of Justice," pp. 104-106; Miller, "Rawls and Marxism," p. 223; and Nagel, "Rawls on Justice," p. 12. Barry, *The Liberal Theory*, p. 104, also criticizes maximin for not guaranteeing a satisfactory minimum.
67. Wolff, *Understanding Rawls*, pp. 69-70. Wolff notes that the requirement to benefit the least well advantaged solves a problem of prioritizing. If the requirement is simply that "all" must benefit, there are possible solutions where everyone would benefit, but where the benefits would be distributed differently. How would the parties choose between such solutions? Requiring that the least advantaged benefit most solves this prioritizing problem (see pp. 39-43). However, it brings other, counterintuitive implications.
68. T. M. Scanlon, "Rawls' Theory of Justice," in *Reading Rawls*, p. 195.
69. Miller, "Rawls and Marxism," p. 214.
70. Barry, *The Liberal Theory*, pp. 16-17.
71. Nozick, *Anarchy, State, and Utopia*, p. 198. Similarly, Wolff, *Understanding Rawls*, p. 207, asserts that the game theory on which Rawls' approach is based is an inadequate model because it "treats the goods to be distributed as exogenously given."
72. Nozick, *Anarchy, State, and Utopia*, p. 198. The question of entitlement is the subject of the next chapter.
73. Ibid., pp. 192-195.
74. Ibid., p. 195. Nagel, *"Rawls on Justice,"* p. 13, makes the same charge.
75. Sandel, *Liberalism*, pp. 78 and 102. Indeed, Sandel argues that at crucial points Rawls depends on a notion of a communal self which he has explicitly rejected. Otherwise, for example, there is no way to defend his notion that our talents and natural attributes are not "ours" but belong in some way to the community (p. 149).
76. Reiman, "The Labor Theory."
77. Barry, *The Liberal Theory*, p. 111.
78. Rawls, *A Theory of Justice*, pp. 157f.; Fishkin, *Justice*, p. 15.

79. Wolff, *Understanding Rawls*, p. 178. Nozick, *Anarchy, State, and Utopia*, p. 203, argues that Rawls' procedure guarantees a focus on end-state principles, since each person calculates his or her probable end-state. The theory therefore prevents derivation of historical, process-oriented principles.

80. As David Lyons, *Forms and Limits of Utilitarianism* (Oxford: Clarendon, 1965), p. 159, puts it, "the contract argument rests upon an unargued commitment to fairness and impartiality."

81. Sandel, *Liberalism*, p. 46. Sandel asserts, "What we need is an account of what exactly constrains the descriptive assumptions appropriate to the initial situation."

82. Ronald Dworkin, "The Original Position," in *Reading Rawls*, p. 19.

83. Sandel, *Liberalism*, p. 119; Lyons, *Forms and Limits*, p. 153, makes a similar comment: "Those principles seem miscast as principles *of justice* even if they can be supported by the argument from rational self-interest."

84. Lyons, *Forms and Limits*, p. 153.

85. Indeed, Hare, "Rawls' Theory of Justice," p. 86, suggests that Rawls is "foisting" a set of moral views on his readers by trying to equate the two.

86. Ibid., p. 84.

87. Lyons, *Forms and Limits*, p. 146.

88. See Dworkin, "The Original Position," p. 24; Lyons, *Forms and Limits*, p. 148; and Wolff, *Understanding Rawls*, pp. 180-191.

89. Wolff, *Understanding Rawls*, p. 195; See also Barber, "Justifying Justice," p. 310.

90. Ackerman, *Social Justice*, p. 336.

91. Wolff, *Understanding Rawls*, p. 7. I concur, though one must also acknowledge the importance of the detailed elaboration of the central insight which Rawls provides in the latter two sections of the book.

92. Wolff (ibid., p. 16) appears to take Rawls' contract method as his central insight. I am more inclined to agree with Nagel that it is the *principles*, and not the contract method per se, that will leave the lasting agenda. See Nagel, "Rawls on Justice," p. 15.

93. Moreover, Rawls would appear to avoid the relativism of other approaches that attempt to be pluralistic. For example, in *Spheres of Justice* (New York: Basic Books, 1983), Michael Walzer argues for a plurality of principles of justice corresponding to different "spheres." There is no central guiding principle (p. 4). However, this leaves the reader wondering why particular practices are chosen as examples of justice in the different spheres and why other practices would not be considered just. Rawls attempts to respond to this sort of relativism by providing a point from which the justice of the basic system can be assessed.

Chapter 3. An Entitlement Alternative: Robert Nozick

1. Robert Nozick, *Anarchy, State, and Utopia* (New York: Basic Books, 1974), p. 153.

2. Ibid., pp. 52-53.

3. Ibid., p. 31. Indeed, he puts it even more strongly in the preface: "Individuals have rights and there are things no person or group may do to them. . ." (p. ix).

4. Ibid., pp. 28-29.

5. H. L. A. Hart, "Between Utility and Rights," in *The Idea of Freedom: Essays in Honour of Isaiah Berlin,* ed. Alan Ryan (Oxford: Oxford University Press, 1979), p. 81.

6. Nozick, *Anarchy, State, and Utopia,* p. 33: "This root idea, namely, that there are different individuals with separate lives and so no one may be sacrificed for others. . .leads to a libertarian side constraint that prohibits aggression against another."

7. Ibid., p. 51.

8. An "invisible hand explanation" shows that something that appears to have been produced by intentional design was in fact brought about by a process that did not have that design in mind (ibid., pp. 19-20).

9. Ibid., p. 11.

10. Ibid., p. 13.

11. Ibid., pp. 22-23.

12. To show that the state is legitimate, says Nozick, one must show (1) that an "ultraminimal" state arises out of the system of protective agencies, (2) that it is transformed into a minimal state, and (3) that each of these moves is morally legitimate (ibid., p. 52).

13. Ibid., p. 56.

14. Ibid., p. 59.

15. Ibid., pp. 63-70.

16. Ibid., p. 71.

17. Ibid., p. 81.

18. What we may do is limited not only by the rights of others, but also by moral considerations about the person acting (some component of knowledge is important) (ibid., pp. 106-107).

19. "It is morally required to [protect all] by the principle of compensation, which requires those who act in self-protection in order to increase their own security to compensate those they prohibit from doing risky acts which might actually have turned out to be harmless" (ibid., p. 114).

20. Ibid., pp. 110f.

21. Ibid., p. 334.

22. Ibid., p. 333.

23. Ibid., p. 27.

24. Ibid., pp. 118-119.

25. Ibid., p. 149.

26. Nozick is not the only one to stress justice in holdings. Although a critic of Nozick on many counts, William Galston asserts that justice has to do with "rightful possession." This is close to Nozick's definition of justice, whatever other differences there may be between the two theorists. See William A. Galston, *Justice and the Human Good* (Chicago: University of Chicago Press, 1980), p. 105.

27. Nozick, *Anarchy, State, and Utopia,* p. 150.

28. Ibid., pp. 161-162.

29. Ibid., p. 163: "No end-state principle or distributional patterned principle of justice can be continuously realized without continuous interference with people's lives."

30. Ibid., pp. 150-152. In addition, there will need to be a principle for rectification of injustice in case either the original holdings or the transfer is not just.
31. Ibid., p. 160. Indeed, Nozick claims that most theories of justice consider only the recipients of goods and not the rights of the givers of goods (p. 168). In this regard it is interesting to recall one of the examples Mill offers for the inadequacy of "justice" to solve difficult issues of distribution. In considering whether remuneration should be given for talent and contribution or for effort (doing the best one can), Mill declares that "the one looks to what it is just that the individual should receive, the other to what it is just that the community should give" (John Stuart Mill, *Utilitarianism* [New York: Bobbs-Merrill, 1957], p. 71).
32. Nozick, *Anarchy, State, and Utopia*, p. 153.
33. Ibid., p. 155.
34. Ibid., p. 157.
35. Hart, "Between Utility and Rights," p. 81.
36. Nozick, *Anarchy, State, and Utopia*, p. 175.
37. Ibid., pp. 178-179. However, Nozick limits the "hurt" here to the damage done because others can no longer "use" the thing; their inability to acquire it themselves is a permissible hurt, in his view.
38. Ibid., p. 180.
39. Ibid., p. 178.
40. Ibid., p. 181.
41. Ibid., pp. 177-178.
42. Ibid., p. 167. Nozick does allow one possible role for such patterned principles. He suggests that a principle such as Rawls' "difference principle" might serve as a "rough rule of thumb" for approximating the principle of rectification in places where acquisition and transfer have not been fair (p. 231).
43. Ibid., p. 169.
44. Ibid., p. 172. The value-laden nature of Nozick's language here and elsewhere in the book should be noted.
45. Ibid., p. 230.
46. See James S. Fishkin, *Justice, Equal Opportunity, and the Family* (New Haven: Yale University Press, 1983), p. 13.
47. Hart, "Between Utility and Rights," p. 81.
48. In a well-known passage, Nozick says: "Individually, we each sometimes choose to undergo some pain or sacrifice for a greater benefit or to avoid a greater harm. . . . Why not, *similarly*, hold that some persons have to bear some costs that benefit other persons more, for the sake of the overall social good. But there is no *social entity*. . . . There are only individual people. . . . Using one of these people for the benefit of others, uses him and benefits the others. Nothing more" (*Anarchy, State, and Utopia*, p. 130).
49. Cf. Galston, *Justice*, and Michael Walzer, *Spheres of Justice: A Defense of Pluralism and Equality* (New York: Basic Books, 1983).
50. Fishkin, *Justice*, p. 135.
51. Nozick, *Anarchy, State, and Utopia*, p. 182.
52. Hart, "Between Utility and Rights," p. 85.
53. G. A. Cohen, "Capitalism, Freedom and the Proletariat," in *The Idea of Freedom*, pp. 10-11.
54. Ibid., p. 15.

55. Ibid.
56. Ibid., p. 13.
57. Hart, "Between Utility and Rights," p. 85.
58. Bruce A. Ackerman, *Social Justice in the Liberal State* (New Haven: Yale University Press, 1980), p. 186. Ackerman's own proposal for a liberal approach depends on notions of "neutral dialogue" in which rights are not preexistent but emerge out of a carefully constrained dialog. The primary constraint is that no one is permitted to claim superiority to others.
59. Walzer, *Spheres of Justice,* p. 119.
60. Ibid., p. 22.
61. Jon P. Gunnemann, "Capitalism and Commutative Justice," in the 1985 *Annual of the Society of Christian Ethics,* ed. Alan Anderson.
62. Ackerman, *Social Justice,* p. 188.
63. Walzer, *Spheres of Justice,* p. 119.
64. Emil Brunner, *Justice and the Social Order* (London: Lutterworth, 1945), p. 161.
65. John P. Langan, s.j., "Rawls, Nozick, and the Search for Social Justice," *Theological Studies* 38 (1977): 357.
66. Brunner, *Justice,* p. 134.
67. Ibid.
68. Nozick, *Anarchy, State, and Utopia,* p. 237.
69. At another point, Nozick uses the example of grading to show that there are entitlements (ibid., p. 199). Walzer clearly distinguishes norms for justice in the assignment or grades or prizes from norms for justice in the economic arena.
70. Fishkin, *Justice,* p. 136, n. 36.
71. Hart, "Between Utility and Rights," p. 85. The argument here is reminiscent of Daniels' challenge to Rawls that liberty without "worth of liberty" is not liberty at all. See Norman Daniels, "Equal Liberty and Unequal Worth of Liberty," in *Reading Rawls.*
72. Galston, *Justice,* p. 230. Indeed, Galston and others would argue that *need* is a fundamental claim precisely because of the close connection between need and harm (p. 199).
73. Langan, "Rawls," p. 357.
74. Walzer, *Spheres of Justice,* p. 74.
75. Fishkin, *Justice,* pp. 4-6, 159. Fishkin (p. 83) therefore proposes that we have a "trilemma"—a three-legged stool whose legs cannot stand together. He calls contemporary liberalism an "incoherent ideal" for public policy.
76. See, for example, Nicholas Rescher's careful distinction between claims and entitlements, and his arguments for need and desert in *Distributive Justice* (New York: Bobbs-Merrill, 1966).

Chapter 4. A Catholic Response: The National Conference of Catholic Bishops

1. National Conference of Catholic Bishops, *Pastoral Letter on Catholic Social Teaching and the U.S. Economy,* second draft (Washington, D.C., October 7, 1985), hereafter cited as "Bishops' Letter"; numbers in the text are given. The third draft of the letter was published while this book was in press.
2. Bishops' Letter, 32.

3. In spite of the fact that the bishops' letter is entitled "Catholic Social Teaching and the U.S. Economy," nowhere does it review Catholic social teaching or offer a summary of that teaching. The summary offered here is my own. Recent papal and conciliar documents can be found in Joseph Gremillion, *The Gospel of Peace and Justice: Catholic Social Teaching since Pope John* (Maryknoll, N.Y.: Orbis, 1976); earlier encyclicals are published as pamphlets by the Daughters of St. Paul (Boston).

4. J. Bryan Hehir, "John Paul II: Continuity and Change in the Social Teaching of the Church," in *Co-Creation and Capitalism: John Paul II's* Laborem Exercens, ed. John W. Houch and Oliver F. Williams (Lanham, Md.: University Press of America, 1983), p. 124.

5. Hehir, ibid., pp. 125-126, finds three stages. The first, from Leo XIII through Pius XII, focused on economic justice within the nation. The second, from Pius XII to Paul VI, focused on international questions and lifted up human rights as a theme. The third, beginning with Paul VI's *Octogesima Adveniens* and continuing through the present, has kept the international focus but added concern for new changes within the nation, such as urbanization and the development of mass communications.

6. David Hollenbach, s.j., *Claims in Conflict: Retrieving and Renewing the Catholic Human Rights Tradition* (New York: Paulist, 1979), p. 62, suggests that the years of John XXIII and Vatican II constitute a watershed in the tradition.

7. For the former position, see Leo XIII, *Rerum Novarum* (1891), §23; for the latter, see Paul VI, *Populorum Progressio* (1967) §§23, 24.

8. Charles E. Curran attributes these three affirmations to the great American Catholic ethicist John A. Ryan. See Curran, *American Catholic Social Ethics: Twentieth Century Approaches* (Notre Dame: University of Notre Dame Press, 1982), p. 61. However, Ryan was a man of his tradition, and these three statements serve as well as a summary of basic affirmations underlying papal and conciliar documents during this period.

9. Hollenbach, *Claims in Conflict*, p. 42, says, "The thread that ties all these documents together is their common concern for the protection of the dignity of the human person."

10. *Rerum Novarum* §63. The sentiment was echoed by John XXIII when he declared that workers must receive a wage "sufficient to lead a life worthy of man. . ." (*Mater et Magistra* 1961, §71).

11. The phrase "living wage" can be attributed to John A. Ryan; the concept, however, was clearly present in *Rerum Novarum*, and has continued to permeate the tradition. More recently, phrases such as "family wage" are used. See Pope John Paul II, *Laborem Exercens* (1981), §19.

12. *Quadragesimo Anno* (1931), part II, section 5.

13. Ibid., part III, section 1. John XXIII, *Mater et Magistra*, §71, echoed this concern for accumulation of economic power: "just as remuneration for work cannot be left entirely to unregulated competition, neither may it be decided arbitrarily at the will of the more powerful."

14. *Populorum Progressio,* §§58-59.

15. *Justice in the World* (1971), §§3, 16.

16. John Paul II, in *Laborem Exercens,* §20, declared that unions are a "mouthpiece for the struggle for social justice."

17. *Quadragesimo Anno*, §34.
18. *Mater et Magistra*, §73. He called it a "strict demand of social justice."
19. *Gaudium et Spes* (1965), §§67 and 65.
20. *Populorum Progressio*, §14.
21. *Octogesima Adveniens* (1971), §22. The 1971 Synod of Bishops summarized this trend by declaring that "economic injustice and lack of social participation keep a [person] from attaining his [or her] basic human and civil rights" (*Justice in the World*, §9).
22. A rather complete listing of rights is provided by Pope John XXIII in *Pacem in Terris* (1963), §§11-27. "The right to take an active part in public affairs and to contribute one's part to the common good" is explicitly mentioned (§26).
23. John XXIII, *Mater et Magistra*, §83.
24. Cf. Leo XIII, *Rerum Novarum*, §§10 and 19; John XXIII, *Mater et Magistra*, §§109 and 71.
25. *Rerum Novarum*, §35.
26. Ibid., §36.
27. *Quadragesimo Anno*, part II, section 1.
28. *Gaudium et Spes*, §69.
29. *Populorum Progressio*, §24.
30. Ibid., §22.
31. Pius XI, *Quadragesimo Anno*, part II, section 4.
32. John XXIII, *Mater et Magistra*, §71.
33. John Paul II, *Laborem Exercens*, §12.
34. *Rerum Novarum*, §§5, 6.
35. *Quadragesimo Anno*, part II, section 3.
36. *Mater et Magistra*, §140.
37. *Gaudium et Spes*, §29.
38. Pius XI, *Quadragesimo Anno*, part II, section 3. In *Mater et Magistra* John XXIII extends the principle to the obligation of the rich nations to help the poor (§161).
39. *Octogesimo Anno*, §23. See Donal Dorr, *Option for the Poor: A Hundred Years of Vatican Social Teaching* (Maryknoll, N.Y.: Orbis, 1983). Dorr argues, however, that the very explicit meaning of this phrase, which has emerged with liberation theology, has not always been present in Catholic tradition.
40. *Rerum Novarum*, §54. See also *Pacem in Terris*, §56.
41. John XXIII was particularly prone to this form of reasoning. See, for example, *Mater et Magistra*, §150: "justice and equity demand. . ."; §161: "justice and humanity require. . ."; §168: "necessity and justice require. . . ."
42. *Gaudium et Spes*, §63.
43. *Justice in the World*, §§30-31.
44. *Octogesimo Anno*, §23.
45. John Paul II gives voice to this belief in social consensus by rejecting any assumptions that labor and capital are "opposed" to each other. A labor system can be "right," he asserts, only if "in its very basis it overcomes the opposition between capital and labor" (*Laborem Exercens*, §13). This is an explicit rejection of Marxist assumptions regarding the forces of capitalism.
46. The phrase *rigid capitalism* is used by John Paul II, and refers to "the position that defends the exclusive right to private ownership of the means of production as an untouchable 'dogma' of economic life" (*Laborem Exercens*, §14).

47. Bishops' Letter, 49; emphasis in the original.
48. Ibid., 1.
49. Ibid., 28; in the first draft of this letter, the bishops were even more forceful on this issue: "*Our fundamental norm is this: Will this decision or policy help the poor and deprived members of the human community and enable them to become more active participants in economic life?*" (21; emphasis in the original).
50. Ibid., 120.
51. Ibid., 22.
52. Ibid., 28.
53. At several points, the bishops declare that the religious understanding is "supported" by philosophical reflection and common human experience; see ibid., 34, 67.
54. Ibid., 36.
55. Ibid., 38.
56. Ibid., 40.
57. Ibid., 45, 43.
58. Ibid., 44.
59. Ibid., 47.
60. Ibid., 49-51.
61. Ibid., 58. The bishops stress that early Christianity did not therefore "canonize" poverty; poverty is always cause for sadness.
62. Ibid., 59.
63. Ibid., 67.
64. Ibid., 73.
65. For helpful background on the Catholic tradition on justice, see Josef Pieper, *The Four Cardinal Virtues* (Notre Dame: Notre Dame University Press, 1966), and especially David Hollenbach, s.j., "Modern Catholic Teaching Concerning Justice," in *The Faith that Does Justice*, ed. John C. Haughey (New York: Paulist, 1977).
66. Bishops' Letter, 74.
67. Ibid., 75.
68. Ibid., 76-78. The bishops simply assert that distributive justice requires allocation in light of unmet basic material needs. No philosophical arguments for this stress on need are offered, although its grounding in Scripture is implied in the previous discussion.
69. Ibid., 81; emphasis in the original.
70. Ibid.
71. Ibid., 83.
72. Ibid., 92.
73. Ibid., 93. Again, the bishops seem to have drawn back from their first draft, where they declared flatly that increasing participation takes precedence over "privileged concentrations of power, wealth, and income" (104).
74. Ibid., 94.
75. Ibid., 95.
76. Ibid., 132-133.
77. Ibid., 97-102. The bishops here draw on Pope John Paul II's *Laborem Exercens*, in which he argued that work was both a right and a duty.
78. Ibid., 135: "Full employment is the foundation of a just economy."

79. Ibid., 140-142. As might be expected, the bishops urge that "what we can least afford is the assault on human dignity" (142).
80. Ibid., 152, 153.
81. Ibid., 157-168. The bishops' specific policy recommendations remain rather general and have the air of urging rather than specifying action.
82. Ibid., 108. More will be said about their implicit acceptance of capitalism in the critique, below.
83. Ibid., 113.
84. Ibid., 102.
85. Ibid., 113.
86. Ibid., 169-182.
87. Ibid., 181.
88. Ibid., 183: "Some degree of inequality is not only acceptable, but may be considered desirable for economic and social reasons."
89. Ibid.
90. Ibid., 186.
91. Ibid., 192.
92. Ibid., 194-211. The bishops make several specific recommendations here, e.g., that welfare benefits should be available for two-parent families, that a national welfare minimum should be established, and others.
93. See, e.g., Peter M. Flanigan, "The Pastoral and the Letter," and Edward L. Hennessy Jr., "A Pastoral for the Poor, Not the Economy," both in *America,* January 12, 1985. These were part of a series of essays on the Bishops' Letter in *America* during spring 1985. See also David A. Krueger, "Bishops, Business, and the Unfinished Task," *Christian Century,* July 3-10, 1985.
94. See, e.g., Flanigan, "The Pastoral," and Michael Novak, "Toward Consensus: Suggestions for Revising the First Draft, Part I," *Catholicism in Crisis,* March 1985. Both Flanigan and Novak were involved in the publication of a Catholic Lay Commission letter entitled "Toward the Future," which predated the first draft of the bishops' pastoral and attempted to anticipate criticism of the pastoral.
95. Krueger, "Bishops," p. 639.
96. Flanigan, "The Pastoral," p. 13. Novak, "Toward Consensus," p. 14, also notes that the poor could be lifted out of poverty without affecting disparities in wealth; he suggests that the bishops have a hidden agenda in linking the fact of inequality of income to the fact of poverty.
97. Novak, "Toward Consensus," pp. 14-15.
98. Ibid., pp. 12, 13.
99. Ibid., p. 13. But see Hennessy, "A Pastoral," p. 17, who argues that the best hope for the poor is the creation of jobs. Critics appear to be trying to have it both ways at this point: on the one hand, they urge that the best way to overcome poverty is through a strong economy that creates jobs; on the other hand, they urge that "economic participation" is not an acceptable norm, because most of the poor are not capable of having jobs!
100. Novak, "Toward Consensus," p. 9; Flanigan, "The Pastoral," p. 14.
101. Novak, "Toward Consensus," p. 11.
102. Ibid., p. 8; Flanigan, "The Pastoral," p. 14.
103. Flanigan, "The Pastoral," p. 14.
104. Novak, "Toward Consensus," pp. 9, 11.

105. Ibid., p. 8; Bishops' Letter, 28.
106. Bishops' Letter, 194.
107. Bishops' Letter, first draft (published in *Origins* 14 [November 1984]), 21.
108. Bishops' Letter, 28.
109. Bishops' Letter, first draft, 104.
110. Bishops' Letter, 93. The dropping of the phrase regarding priority over privilege may be a response to Flanigan, who argued that a free economy does not preserve privilege and that the bishops appeared to be setting the rich against the poor in ways that were unduly divisive ("The Pastoral," p. 13). Novak also raised the challenge that any "privilege" was notoriously difficult to document ("Toward Consensus," pp. 13-14).
111. Bishops' Letter, 81.
112. Ibid., 92-93. One might also ask whether the bishops were truly willing to follow up the implications of "participation" within the Catholic church, which still denies ordination to women. Larry Rasmussen, "Economic Policy: Creation, Covenant, and Community," *America,* May 4, 1985, p. 367, challenges the church to practice what it preaches by institutionalizing a new economic experiment within its own ranks; "*that* would influence public policy," he declares.
113. Beverly W. Harrison, "Social Justice and Economic Orthodoxy," *Christianity and Crisis,* January 21, 1985, p. 514.
114. Bishops' Letter, 127.
115. Ibid., 128.
116. Ibid., 129.
117. Ibid., 113.
118. For example, ibid., 22: "Both Christian conviction and the promise of this nation to secure liberty and justice for all imply that the poor and vulnerable have a special claim on our concern."
119. Gregory Baum, "A Canadian Perspective on the U.S. Pastoral," *Christianity and Crisis,* January 21, 1985, pp. 517-518.
120. Rasmussen, "Economic Policy," p. 367, suggested, for example, that the first draft "vacillated" between an approach that simply "mainstreamed" the poor and an approach that called for structural change.
121. Donal Dorr, *Option for the Poor,* pp. 131, 135f., makes this charge of much of recent Catholic social teaching.
122. Vincent A. Carrafiello, "Bishops Lash U.S. Economic Policy," *The Month,* February, 1985.
123. Harrison, "Social Justice," p. 515. Failure to take a global perspective weakened the theoretical base for the policy implications, in Harrison's view.
124. Rasmussen, "Economic Policy," p. 366.
125. The term *option for the poor* has become popular in liberation theology. Donal Dorr, *Option for the Poor,* pp. 3-4, suggests that it means minimally a focus on structural injustice that recognizes the ways in which economic, political, cultural, and religious structures maintain and promote the dominance of the rich over the poor and that commits itself to being in solidarity with the poor in their struggles for justice.
126. Harrison, "Social Justice," p. 513; see Chap. 6, below.
127. The term appears for the first time in the Bishops' Letter in §62.
128. Bishops' Letter, 90.

129. Hollenbach, *Claims in Conflict,* pp. 109-123, notes, for example, that neoscholastic thought had great confidence in human reason. This confidence was the "object of Protestant theological criticism." In the post-Vatican II tradition, this confidence has weakened, and the tradition now recognizes the need for faith in discernment.
130. Carrafiello, "Bishops."
131. *Octogesima Adveniens,* §4.
132. Friendly critic Robert Lekachman, "The Bishops Offend the Secular Hierarchy," *Christianity and Crisis,* January 21, 1985, p. 508, suggests that, minimally, the appeal to "Catholic conscience" should be "reinforced by an appeal to Catholic self-interest."
133. Harvey Cox, "Imagining an Economy Based on Shalom," *Christianity and Crisis,* January 21, 1985, p. 510.
134. Bishops' Letter, 60.
135. Cox, "Imagining," p. 510.
136. Ibid., pp. 510, 512.
137. Bishops' Letter, 67.
138. For example, Protestants John Howard Yoder and Stanley Hauerwas both argue for a more "sectarian" view of Christian ethics that does not depend on "natural law" or "reason" as its base, but stresses the distinctive contributions of Scripture and Christian community. See John Howard Yoder, *The Politics of Jesus* (Grand Rapids: Eerdmans, 1972); and Stanley Hauerwas, *A Community of Character: Toward a Constructive Christian Social Ethic* (Notre Dame: University of Notre Dame Press, 1981).

Chapter 5. A Protestant Alternative: Reinhold Niebuhr

1. See Ronald H. Stone, *Reinhold Niebuhr: Prophet to Politicians* (Nashville: Abingdon, 1972); also John C. Bennett, "Reinhold Niebuhr's Social Ethics," in *Reinhold Niebuhr: His Religious, Social, and Political Thought,* ed. Charles W. Kegley and Robert W. Bretall (New York: Macmillan, 1956). However, there is a core to Niebuhr's ethics. I agree with Bennett in locating that core in the "middle" of Niebuhr's writings—those of the 1930s and 1940s. In view of Niebuhr's later refusal to support "any position" taken in his early work *An Interpretation of Christian Ethics* (see *Reinhold Niebuhr,* ed. Kegley and Bretall, pp. 434-435), I have made use of that volume here only when statements in it are substantially supported by Niebuhr's other writings.
2. Reinhold Niebuhr, *An Interpretation of Christian Ethics* (New York: Seabury, 1979; first published 1935), p. 22.
3. Reinhold Niebuhr, *The Nature and Destiny of Man,* 2 vols. (New York: Scribner, 1943, 1964), vol. 2, *Human Destiny,* p. 73.
4. D. B. Robertson, ed., *Love and Justice: Selections from the Shorter Writings of Reinhold Niebuhr* (Gloucester, Mass.: Peter Smith, 1976), p. 25; Niebuhr, *Nature and Destiny,* 2:244; Reinhold Niebuhr, *The Children of Light and the Children and Darkness* (London: Nisbet, 1945), p. 11.
5. Niebuhr, *Nature and Destiny,* 2, chap. 3.
6. Niebuhr, *Christian Ethics,* p. 100: "The complete identification of life with life which the law of love demands."
7. Robertson, *Love and Justice,* p. 31.

8. Gene Outka, *Agape: An Ethical Analysis* (New Haven: Yale University Press, 1972), p. 169. However, Franklin I. Gamwell, "Reinhold Niebuhr's Theistic Ethic," in *The Legacy of Reinhold Niebuhr*, ed. Nathan A. Scott (Chicago: University of Chicago Press, 1975), p. 68, suggests that these two are not synonymous, as Niebuhr implied. In Gamwell's view, "perfect harmony" can include an affirmation of the interests of the self which is excluded by "self-sacrifice."

9. Niebuhr, *Nature and Destiny*, 2:72.

10. Robertson, *Love and Justice*, p. 27.

11. Niebuhr, *Christian Ethics*, p. 39; cf. Robertson, *Love and Justice*, p. 27.

12. Reinhold Niebuhr, *Nature and Destiny*, vol. 1, *Human Nature*, p. 179; see also p. 140.

13. Reinhold Niebuhr, *Moral Man and Immoral Society* (New York: Scribner, 1932, 1960), p. 117.

14. Niebuhr, *Nature and Destiny*, 1:179. These two forms of sin are never separate, however. Those who wish to justify injustice always claim a kind of superiority for themselves that amounts to idolatry (ibid., p. 166).

15. Robertson, *Love and Justice*, p. 164; cf. Niebuhr, *Nature and Destiny*, 2:252.

16. Cf. Niebuhr's statement that "in. . .distributive justice the self regards itself as an equal but not as a specially privileged member. . ." (*Christian Realism and Political Problems* [New York: Scribner, 1953], p. 160).

17. Robertson, *Love and Justice*, p. 282; cf. Niebuhr, *Christian Ethics*, p. 90.

18. Robertson, *Love and Justice*, p. 30; cf. Niebuhr, *Nature and Destiny*, 2:72: "A love which 'seeketh not its own' is not able to maintain itself in historical society." It should be noted here that Niebuhr understands Jesus to have had primarily a personal ethic in which actions are motivated purely by obedience to God and in disregard of social consequences (Robertson, pp. 30-31).

19. Robertson, *Love and Justice*, p. 212.

20. Niebuhr, *Nature and Destiny*, 2:88; cf. Reinhold Niebuhr, *Moral Man*, p. 267.

21. Robertson, *Love and Justice*, p. 243.

22. Niebuhr, *Moral Man*, p. 75; cf. p. 84: "The selfishness of nations is proverbial." Niebuhr notes that loyalty to the nation is a high form of individual altruism, but that it becomes transmuted into patriotism, which is national egoism. Thus, "the unselfishness of individuals makes for the selfishness of nations" (*Moral Man* p. 91).

23. Cf. Niebuhr, *Moral Man*, p. 213.

24. Niebuhr, *Christian Ethics*, p. 62; *Moral Man*, p. 68; *Nature and Destiny*, 1:295.

25. John Bennett calls Niebuhr's view of love and justice "extraordinarily many-sided" ("Reinhold Niebuhr's Social Ethics," p. 58). M. M. Thomas, "A Third World View of Christian Realism," *Christianity and Crisis*, 46:8 (1986), says that it is characterized by "almost unscrupulous fluctuations."

26. Robertson, *Love and Justice*, p. 25.

27. Niebuhr, *Nature and Destiny*, 2:247.

28. Ibid., p. 252.

29. E.g., Robertson, *Love and Justice*, p. 207: "Some balance of power is the basis of whatever justice is achieved in human relations." Cf. p. 300: "Every historic form of justice has been attained by some equilibrium of power."

30. Ibid., p. 32; cf. Niebuhr, *Moral Man*, p. 258.

31. Robertson, *Love and Justice*, p. 49.

32. Ibid., p. 28.
33. Ibid., p. 162: ". . .Maintaining a relative justice in an evil world."
34. Niebuhr, *Nature and Destiny*, 2:280.
35. Ibid., 2:248.
36. Niebuhr, *Christian Ethics*, pp. 66-67, suggests that there is an "ascending scale" of moral possibilities that more closely approximate love as societies move from the minimum of rights to life and property toward recognition of a fuller set of rights beyond those which are legally enforced.
37. Niebuhr, *Nature and Destiny*, 2:252. Indeed, here Niebuhr says that Marxism is correct in seeing that rules of justice are "primarily rationalizations of the interests of the dominant elements of a society."
38. Niebuhr, *Christian Ethics*, p. 112; *Nature and Destiny*, 1:295.
39. Niebuhr, *Christian Ethics*, pp. 90, 128; *Nature and Destiny*, 1:295.
40. Niebuhr, *Christian Ethics*, p. 85; *Nature and Destiny*, 1:285, 2:246.
41. Niebuhr constantly stresses that there are "higher possibilities of justice in every historic situation" (*Nature and Destiny*, 2:284; see also *Children of Light*, p. 53). Niebuhr eschews consistency and argues that it is "impossible to fix upon a single moral absolute" in historic situations of justice (*Christian Ethics*, p. 121).
42. Robertson, *Love and Justice*, p. 32.
43. Niebuhr, *Nature and Destiny*, 2:254. Indeed, he calls these part of the "absolute natural law" (*Nature and Destiny*, 2:280).
44. Robertson, *Love and Justice*, p. 87.
45. Ibid., p. 95. Gordon Harland, *The Thought of Reinhold Niebuhr* (New York: Oxford University Press, 1960), p. 55, suggests that Niebuhr emphasized liberty increasingly over the years.
46. Niebuhr, *Christian Ethics*, p. 80.
47. Ibid., pp. 65-66; cf. p. 121.
48. Niebuhr, *Nature and Destiny*, 2:254; see also *Christian Ethics*, p. 65: "In the ideal of equality there is an echo of the law of love, 'Thou shalt love thy neighbor *as thyself.*' "
49. Niebuhr, *Moral Man*, p. 171.
50. Cf. Bennett, "Reinhold Niebuhr's Social Ethics," pp. 58-59.
51. Niebuhr, *Children of Light*, p. 55; *Nature and Destiny*, 2:255. Bennett, "Reinhold Niebuhr's Social Ethics," p. 59, suggests that Niebuhr accepted more inequalities in his later years.
52. Niebuhr, *Christian Ethics*, p. 66.
53. Niebuhr, *Moral Man*, p. 234. Roger L. Shinn, "Realism, Radicalism, and Eschatology in Reinhold Niebuhr: A Reassessment," in *The Legacy of Reinhold Niebuhr*, p. 94, notes that although Niebuhr did not think the oppressed were immune from sin, he did see them as in a better position than the powerful to unmask the frauds of society.
54. Niebuhr, *Nature and Destiny*, 2:248.
55. Niebuhr, *Christian Ethics*, p. 125.
56. Niebuhr, *Moral Man*, pp. 30-31.
57. Ibid., p. 32; cf. Niebuhr, *Christian Ethics*, p. 100.
58. Niebuhr, *Moral Man*, p. 237.

59. Niebuhr, *Christian Ethics*, pp. 79f.; Robertson, *Love and Justice*, p. 47; Niebuhr, *Nature and Destiny*, 1:284.
60. Niebuhr, *Nature and Destiny*, 2:252.
61. Robertson, *Love and Justice*, p. 48.
62. Niebuhr, *Nature and Destiny*, 2:214.
63. Niebuhr, *Christian Ethics*, p. 137.
64. Niebuhr, *Moral Man*, p. xiv. In ibid., p. 162, he declares: "Special privileges make all men dishonest. The purest conscience and the clearest mind is prostituted by the desire to prove them morally justified."
65. Ibid., p. 80.
66. Robertson, *Love and Justice*, p. 254.
67. Ibid., p. 207.
68. Niebuhr, *Nature and Destiny*, 2:257.
69. Robertson, *Love and Justice*, p. 52. In Niebuhr's view, two things are necessary for the establishment of social justice: (1) a balance of powers, and (2) a central organizing power. Each of these can become distorted and contradict the law of love—the first by dissolving into anarchy, the second by becoming tyranny (*Nature and Destiny*, 2:257-258).
70. Robertson, *Love and Justice*, p. 173.
71. Ibid., p. 36.
72. Ibid., p. 199; Niebuhr, *Nature and Destiny*, 2:262; cf. *Nature and Destiny*, 1:223; Robertson, *Love and Justice*, pp. 173, 199.
73. Bennett, "Reinhold Niebuhr's Social Ethics," p. 60.
74. Langdon Gilkey, "Reinhold Niebuhr's Theology of History," in *The Legacy of Reinhold Niebuhr*, p. 36.
75. Niebuhr, *Nature and Destiny*, 2:257.
76. Ibid., 2:257-258.
77. Ibid., 2:269; Niebuhr speaks of "both the vice and the necessity of government" (ibid., p. 278).
78. Cf. Stone, *Reinhold Niebuhr*, p. 27; also Richard Kroner, "The Historical Roots of Niebuhr's Thought," in *Reinhold Niebuhr*, ed. Kegley and Bretall, p. 30; also Emil Brunner, "Some Remarks on Reinhold Niebuhr's World as a Christian Thinker," in *Reinhold Niebuhr*, ed. Kegley and Bretall, p. 30.
79. Niebuhr, *Christian Ethics*, p. 113; cf. Niebuhr, *Moral Man*, p. 163. Niebuhr's own beginnings as a pastor in Detroit shaped his sense of the centrality of economic issues; see Stone, *Reinhold Niebuhr*, p. 27.
80. Niebuhr, *Christian Ethics*, p. 113. Niebuhr claimed (*Moral Man*, p. 149) that Marx grasped the essence of capitalistic democracy when he said that "the oppressed are allowed, once every few years, to decide which particular representatives of the oppressing classes are to represent and repress them in politics." See also ibid., p. 210, where he declares that economic power is more basic than political power.
81. Niebuhr, *Nature and Destiny*, 2:262-263.
82. Niebuhr, *Children of Light*, p. 76.
83. Niebuhr, *Christian Ethics*, p. 113.
84. Robertson, *Love and Justice*, p. 46. It should be noted that Niebuhr recognized the difference between modern capitalism and the capitalism of Adam Smith's theory. A dogma intended to guarantee the economic freedom of the individual

became the "ideology" of vast corporate structures and was used to prevent proper control of their power (*Children of Light*, p. 25).

85. Robertson, *Love and Justice*, p. 257; cf. Niebuhr, *Christian Ethics*, p. 90. In early stages, Niebuhr was frankly Marxian in his economic analysis. However, he always argued that Marxists were wrong to think that the socialization of property alone would bring about justice.

86. Robertson, *Love and Justice*, pp. 92-93.

87. Ibid., p. 276; cf. pp. 261 and 53.

88. Niebuhr, *Moral Man*, p. 179. Niebuhr had been a pacifist in his early years, but became disillusioned with pacifists after the First World War.

89. Robertson, *Love and Justice*, p. 38.

90. "It is because men are sinners that justice can be achieved only by a certain degree of coercion on the one hand, and by a resistance to coercion and tyranny on the other hand" (Reinhold Niebuhr, *Christianity and Power Politics* [New York: Scribner, 1946], p. 14).

91. Niebuhr, *Moral Man*, p. 192; cf. *Christian Ethics*, p. 114, where Niebuhr accuses the middle-class church of disavowing "violence" when it is composed of people "who have enough economic and other forms of covert power to be able to dispense with the more overt forms of violence." See also Robertson, *Love and Justice*, p. 255, where he accuses pacifist Quakers of not realizing "to what degree they are the beneficiaries of an essentially violent system."

92. Niebuhr, *Nature and Destiny*, 2:275; governments are particularly condemned, because they "oppressed the poor" (*Nature and Destiny*, 2:269).

93. Robertson, *Love and Justice*, p. 167.

94. Cf. Harland, *Thought*, p. 35.

95. Niebuhr, *Nature and Destiny*, 2:284.

96. Brunner, "Some Remarks," p. 30.

97. Harland, *Thought*, p. 23.

98. Reinhold Niebuhr, "Reply to Interpretation and Criticism," in *Reinhold Niebuhr*, ed. Kegley and Bretall, p. 435. For a contemporary Protestant ethicist who argues much the same in developing a theory of justice, see Stephen Charles Mott, *Biblical Ethics and Social Change* (New York: Oxford University Press, 1982).

99. Cf. Daniel Day Williams, "Niebuhr and Liberalism," in *Reinhold Niebuhr*, ed. Kegley and Bretall, p. 203.

100. See Outka, *Agape*, p. 80.

101. Williams, "Niebuhr and Liberalism," p. 210. The suggestion of Dennis P. McCann, *Christian Realism and Liberation Theology: Practical Theologies in Creative Conflict* (Maryknoll, N.Y.: Orbis, 1981), p. 91, that Niebuhr offers essentially a dispositional ethic, might be helpful here. If "love" and "justice" do not function as norms for Niebuhr, but rather as dispositions, then it is possible to reduce any presumed conflicts, since they no longer represent "requirements" in the social world.

102. Niebuhr, *Moral Man*, p. 57.

103. I am drawing here on several aspects of Outka's analysis (cf. Outka, *Agape*, pp. 80 and 169).

104. Kenneth Thompson, "The Political Philosophy of Reinhold Niebuhr," in *Reinhold Niebuhr*, ed. Kegley and Bretall, p. 173.

105. McCann, *Christian Realism*, p. 124.

106. Outka, *Agape*, p. 120.
107. Harland, *Thought*, p. 28.
108. McCann, *Christian Realism*, p. 103; see also pp. 91-92.
109. Harland, *Thought*, p. 52. Longwood attempts to relate Niebuhr's theory to traditional categories such as need, merit, and rank. He argues that Niebuhr clearly permits some inequalities on the basis of both need and rank. See Merle Longwood, "Niebuhr and a Theory of Justice," *Dialog* 14 (1985): 253-262.
110. Bennett, "Reinhold Niebuhr's Social Ethics," p. 57.
111. Paul Ramsey, "Love and Law," in *Reinhold Niebuhr*, ed. Kegley and Bretall, p. 83.
112. Niebuhr, *Moral Man*, p. 155; one could add endless examples!
113. Robertson, *Love and Justice*, p. 196.
114. Ibid., p. 257.
115. Ibid., p. 146.
116. Ibid., pp. 99-100.
117. Niebuhr, *Christian Ethics*, p. 121.
118. Niebuhr, *Moral Man*, p. 160.
119. Ibid., p. 128.
120. Ibid., p. 125.
121. Niebuhr, *Children of Light*, p. 64.
122. Robertson, *Love and Justice*, pp. 95f.
123. Herbert O. Edwards, "Niebuhr, 'Realism' and Civil Rights in America," *Christianity and Crisis* 46:13-14, February 1986.
124. M. M. Thomas, "A Third World View of Christian Realism," *Christianity and Crisis* 46:8 (1986).
125. Cf. Isabel Carter Heyward, *The Redemption of God* (Washington, D. C.: University Press of America, 1982), p. 161; the Mudflower Collective (Katie G. Cannon et al.), *God's Fierce Whimsy* (New York: Pilgrim, 1985), p. 91.
126. Outka, *Agape*, p. 43. Numerous critics join Outka. John Bennett, "Christian Realism: A Symposium," *Christianity and Crisis* 28 (August 5, 1968), p. 176, suggests that Niebuhr may have neglected the extent to which history can be influenced by redemptive events. A similar view is voiced by Cox and Geyer in the same symposium. See also Alexander J. Burnstein, "Niebuhr, Scripture, and Normative Judaism," in *Reinhold Niebuhr*, ed. Kegley and Bretall.
127. Bennett, "Christian Realism," p. 176. See also Abraham I. Heschel, "A Hebrew Evaluation of Reinhold Niebuhr," in *Reinhold Niebuhr*, ed. Kegley and Bretall, pp. 394-395.
128. Henry Nelson Wieman, "A Religious Naturalist Looks at Reinhold Niebuhr," in *Reinhold Niebuhr*, ed. Kegley and Bretall, p. 346.
129. For critiques of Niebuhr's understanding and use of reason, see Paul Tillich, "Reinhold Niebuhr's Doctrine of Knowledge," and Henry Nelson Wieman, "A Religious Naturalist." Niebuhr himself refutes Tillich's interpretation in his "Reply to Interpretation and Criticism," in the same volume. Though Niebuhr is critical of the distortions of reason, his view of its role in social ethics does include some positive aspects, as noted above. This criticism therefore seems less important to me than the question whether love is directly applicable to the social arena.

130. John Howard Yoder, *The Politics of Jesus* (Grand Rapids: Eerdmans, 1972), p. 16, n. 7.
131. Ibid., p. 111, n. 12.
132. Just as Niebuhr limits the cross to "self-sacrificial love," however, so Yoder appears to limit its significance to nonviolence. Niebuhr argues in numerous places that Jesus' ethic is better understood as "nonresistance" than as nonviolence.
133. Robertson, *Love and Justice,* p. 39.
134. Yoder's critique was made after Niebuhr's death. However, Stone suggests something along these lines (*Reinhold Niebuhr,* pp. 78-79).
135. Wieman, "A Religious Naturalist," p. 339.
136. E. A. Burtt, "Some Questions about Niebuhr's Theology," in *Reinhold Niebuhr,* ed. Kegley and Bretall, p. 363.
137. Frederick Herzog, *Justice Church* (Maryknoll, N.Y.: Orbis, 1981), p. 109.
138. Gamwell, "Theistic Ethic," p. 77.
139. McCann, *Christian Realism,* p. 117.
140. Ibid., p. 127.
141. Stone, *Reinhold Niebuhr,* p. 240.
142. James Gustafson, *Christian Ethics and the Community* (New York: Pilgrim, 1971), p. 31.
143. Heschel, "A Hebrew Evaluation," p. 392.
144. Stone, *Reinhold Niebuhr,* p. 231.
145. Shinn, "Realism, Radicalism, and Eschatology," p. 87.
146. Stone, *Reinhold Niebuhr,* p. 241. Ill health in his last two decades prevented Niebuhr from traveling to the Third World to gain the first-hand experience that was often his impetus in ethics.

Chapter 6. A Liberation Challenge: Jose Porfirio Miranda

1. Jose Porfirio Miranda, *Marx and the Bible: A Critique of the Philosophy of Oppression* (Maryknoll, N.Y.: Orbis, 1974).
2. Cf. Enrique Dussel, *Ethics and the Theology of Liberation* (Maryknoll, N.Y.: Orbis, 1978), p. 165. Note, however, that Allan Aubrey Boesak, *Farewell to Innocence* (Maryknoll, N.Y.: Orbis, 1977), p. 16, gives credit to James Cone as the first black theologian to focus on liberation as the central message of the gospel.
3. Cf. Juan Luis Segundo, "Capitalism-Socialism: A Theological Crux," *Concilium* 6 (1974): 105.
4. Ernesto Cardinal, "The Gospel in Solentiname," *Concilium* 5 (May 1974): 107, here quotes a woman identified as "Rebecca."
5. Dussel, *Ethics,* p. 2.
6. Boesak, *Farewell,* p. 12: "Theology is passionately involved."
7. In the quote above, Gutierrez stresses reflection on *faith* from the perspective given in praxis. However, elsewhere, é.g., in *The Power of the Poor in History* (Maryknoll, N.Y.: Orbis, 1983), p. 79, he stresses reflection on *practice* in the light of faith.
8. Ibid., p. 37.
9. Ibid., pp. 137, 193. In *A Theology of Liberation* (Maryknoll, N.Y.: Orbis, 1973), p. 291, Gutierrez reviews the various biblical applications of the term *poor* to

the beggar, the weak one, the one bent over or laboring under a weight. Dussel, *Ethics*, pp. 36-37, offers three categories of the poor: the oppressed, the servants or prophets, and those outside the system. The Third General Conference of the Latin American Episcopate at Puebla in 1979 named a range of victims of institutionalized injustice: young children whose chances for development are blocked, laborers ill-paid and kept from organizing, old people disregarded because they are not productive, etc. (§§31-40). Any of these would qualify as poor here. The final document from Puebla can be found in *Puebla and Beyond*, ed. John Eagleson and Philip Sharper (Maryknoll, N.Y.: Orbis, 1979).

10. Gutierrez, *Power of the Poor*, p. 50.

11. These two circumstances take different forms in different contexts where liberation theology is emerging, but they remain constant elements.

12. Black South African theologian Allan Aubrey Boesak, *Farewell*, p. 29, gives a parallel description of his situation: "This is the situation in which black people find themselves. Slavery, domination, injustice; being forced to live a life of contradiction and estrangement in their own country and 'in exile,' where fear and the urge to survive made deception a way of life; being denied a sense of belonging; discrimination—all these were realities which have almost completely broken down the sense of worth of black personhood."

13. Gutierrez, *Theology*, p. 89.

14. Gutierrez, *Power*, p. 93.

15. Ibid., pp. 84, 192. For an excellent introduction to these issues, see Penny Lernoux, "The Long Path to Puebla," in *Puebla and Beyond*.

16. Gutierrez, *Theology*, p. 84.

17. Dussel, *Ethics*, p. 26.

18. See, e.g., reports from the Second General Conference of the Latin American Episcopate at Medellin, 1968, in *The Gospel of Peace and Justice: Catholic Social Teaching since Pope John*, ed. Joseph Gremillion (Maryknoll, N.Y.: Orbis, 1976).

19. The exact form of such grass-roots communities differs from context to context. Note also that Ferm suggests that liberation theology is "rice-roots" theology in the Asian context; Deane William Ferm, "Outlining Rice-Roots Theology," *Christian Century* 101 (January 1984), pp. 78-80.

20. Gutierrez, *Theology*, p. 133.

21. Gutierrez, *Power*, p. 92.

22. Gutierrez, *Theology*, p. 273.

23. Ibid., p. 87.

24. Gutierrez, *Power*, p. 117.

25. Gutierrez, *Theology*, p. 174.

26. Boesak, *Farewell*, p. 34.

27. Gutierrez, *Theology*, p. 88.

28. "Beyond—or rather, through—the struggle against misery, injustice, and exploitation the goal is *the creation of a new man*" (ibid., p. 146).

29. Dussel, *Ethics*, p. 2.

30. An extensive discussion of the hermeneutic of suspicion is provided by Juan Luis Segundo, *Liberation of Theology* (Maryknoll, N.Y.: Orbis, 1976), Chap. 1. Dussel, *Ethics*, p. 166, suggests that what is needed is a "suspicionometer."

31. Jose Miguez Bonino, *Toward a Christian Political Ethic* (Philadelphia: Fortress, 1983), p. 32.
32. Dussel, *Ethics,* p. 43. However, though almost all liberation theologians would join Dussel in urging a different moral judgment on the violence perpetrated by oppressors and that perpetrated in response by the oppressed, not all would support violent revolution.
33. Gutierrez, *Power,* p. 45.
34. Ibid., p. 197.
35. Gutierrez, *Theology,* p. 168.
36. Ibid., p. 195.
37. What distinguishes Miranda's work is, first, his explicit intention to defend Marxist theory, in contrast to many liberation theologians who criticize that theory; and, second, his explicit focus on modes of thinking.
38. Gutierrez, *Theology,* p. 114.
39. Ibid., p. 174.
40. Gutierrez, *Power,* pp. 18, 54.
41. Ibid., p. 117.
42. Ibid., p. 44; cf. p. 155.
43. Ibid., p. 192.
44. Miranda, *Marx,* p. xx.
45. Ibid., p. 2.
46. Gutierrez, *Power,* p. 85.
47. For Gutierrez (see ibid., p. 133) Puebla's attack on the appropriation of wealth by a privileged minority lays the groundwork for a denunciation of the capitalist system and of the presence of multinational corporations.
48. Miranda, *Marx,* p. 7.
49. Ibid., p. 8.
50. Ibid., p. 5-6.
51. Ibid., pp. 10-11.
52. Ibid., p. 14.
53. Ibid., p. 11; it is no surprise that the "comunidades de base" in which liberation theology is emerging tend to be sympathetic to forms of socialism. See Gutierrez, *Theology,* p. 112.
54. Dussel, *Ethics,* p. 25. He argues (ibid., p. 49) that a piece of land measuring a thousand square miles cannot be "natural" private property.
55. Miranda, *Marx,* p. 15.
56. Miranda, quoting Ambrose (ibid., p. 16; emphasis in Miranda).
57. Ibid., p. 19. Miranda suggests that when the popes defend private property it is because they assume it can be acquired legitimately—and even so they set limits on its use and accumulation. The presumption about legitimate acquisition is, of course, rebuttable.
58. Ibid., p. 35. In his review of *Marx and the Bible* (*Journal of Biblical Literature* 94 [1975]:280-281), John L. McKenzie says that the thesis of Miranda's work is that Marxism is what the Bible is seeking. Note, however that Miranda explicitly rejects the notion that he is attempting to make Marx and the Bible coincide (*Marx,* p. 35).
59. Gutierrez, *Power,* p. 211.

60. Indeed, considerable attention is being put into new methods of interpretation of Scripture. The hermeneutical (interpretive) task is central. See, for example, Segundo, *Liberation,* and Elizabeth Schussler-Fiorenza, *In Memory of Her: A Feminist Theological Reconstruction of Christian Origins* (New York: Crossroad, 1984).

61. Miranda, *Marx,* p. 45.

62. Dussel, *Ethics,* p. 176. Note that this epistemology is consonant with the praxis method.

63. Miranda, *Marx,* p. 77; cf. Gutierrez, *Power,* p. 7: "Liberation. . . is the meaning of Yahweh's interventions in history." The term *Yahweh* (or YHWH) is the transliteration of the personal name of God in the Hebrew Scriptures; it is often rendered LORD in English versions.

64. Miranda, *Marx,* p. 78.

65. Ibid., p. 86.

66. Ibid., pp. 88f. Miranda emphasizes that the same God who rescues the oppressed is outraged against the oppressors. Thus, for him liberation and judgment go together (see pp. 47, 100-103). The emphasis on God's wrath against oppressors is somewhat distinctive to Miranda and therefore is not elaborated here.

67. Boesak, *Ethics,* p. 19.

68. Miranda, *Marx,* p. 112.

69. Ibid., p. 127. Miranda is here quoting biblical scholar Hertzberg.

70. Ibid., p. 128.

71. Gutierrez, *Theology,* p. 158.

72. Miranda, *Marx,* pp. 176-182.

73. Gutierrez, *Power,* p. 8. Indeed, the Exodus becomes central, and the creation and covenant are interpreted in light of it. This is in contrast, e.g., to the bishops' statement, in which the Exodus sets the stage for the central theme of covenant.

74. Gutierrez, *Power,* p. 13.

75. Ibid., pp. 95, 116, and 141.

76. Ibid., p. 8. At this point we see how deeply the National Conference of Catholic Bishops was influenced by liberation theology, since it follows suit by making the poor the litmus test of justice. However, there are some important nuances of difference.

77. Bonino, *Toward a Christian Political Ethic,* p. 85: "When God liberates Israel, when he protects the unprotected, when he delivers the captive or vindicates the right of the poor, he is exhibiting his justice."

78. Miranda, *Marx,* p. 99.

79. Boesak, *Farewell,* p. 19.

80. Ibid., p. 125: "The new black refuses to speak of love separated from justice" (see also pp. 4, 146).

81. Dussel, *Ethics,* p. 46.

82. Miranda, *Marx,* p. 61.

83. Gutierrez, *Theology,* p. 106; cf. *Power,* p. 14.

84. Gutierrez, *Theology,* p. 235.

85. Ibid., p. 110.

86. Gutierrez, *Power,* p. 61.

87. Ibid., pp. 7, 14; emphasis added.

152   NOTES

88. Bonino, *Toward a Christian Political Ethic*, p. 85; cf. Carter Heyward, *Our Passion for Justice: Images of Power, Sexuality and Liberation* (New York: Pilgrim, 1984), p. 30: "The Bible as a whole speaks of justice as 'right-relationship' between and among people."
89. Miranda, *Marx*, p. 168.
90. Dennis P. McCann, *Christian Realism and Liberation Theology: Practical Theologies in Creative Conflict* (Maryknoll, N.Y.: Orbis, 1981), p. 137. In an essay on both Gutierrez and his critic Michael Novak, McCann, "Liberation and the Multinationals," *Theology Today* 41 (1984): 54, charges that "for all their appeals to a sense of history, neither provides so much as a paragraph detailing the operations of any specific transnational corporation. . . ." Note, however, that in a content study of liberation theology, J. Emmette Weir, "The Bible and Marx," *Scottish Journal of Theology* 35 (1982): 340, claims that a "significant portion"— as much as 12%—is devoted to a concrete analysis of the situation.
91. See Edward Norman, *Christianity and the World Order* (Oxford: Oxford University Press, 1979), p. 57; see also Peter Hebblethwaite's review of *Marx and the Bible*, in *Religion in Communist Lands* 5 (1977): 257. Bonino, *Toward a Christian Political Ethic*, pp. 94-95, provides a preliminary attempt to understand mechanisms and types of power.
92. Vitor Westhelle, "Dependency Theory: Some Implications for Liberation Theology," *Dialog* 20 (1981): 293-299.
93. Cf. Elisabeth Schüssler-Fiorenza, *Bread, Not Stone: The Challenge of Feminist Biblical Interpretation* (Boston: Beacon, 1984), p. 44: "If liberation theologians make the 'option for the oppressed' the key to their theological endeavors, then they must articulate that 'the oppressed' are women." For an excellent discussion of those particular oppressions, see Rosemary Radford Ruether, "A Feminist Perspective," in Virginia Fabella and Sergio Torres, eds., *Doing Theology in a Divided World* (Maryknoll, N.Y.: Orbis, 1985), pp. 65-71.
94. Reported by McCann, "Liberation," pp. 52-53.
95. McKenzie, *JBL* 94: 280.
96. James M. Wall, "Liberation Ethics: Insisting on Equality," *Christian Century* 99 (November 10, 1982): 1123.
97. J. Deotis Roberts, "Liberation Theologies: A Critical Essay," *Journal of the Interdenominational Theological Center* 9 (Fall 1981): 88. Cf. Michael Novak, "Reinhold Niebuhr: Model for Neoconservatives," *Christian Century* 103 (January 22, 1986): 69-71.
98. Carl E. Braaten, *The Apostolic Imperative* (Minneapolis: Augsburg, 1985), pp. 101-102. This seems to me a clear misreading of liberation theology. As noted above, liberation theology does not ignore liberation from sin.
99. Thomas G. Sanders, "The Theology of Liberation: Christian Utopianism," *Christianity and Crisis* 33:15 (1973): 169. However, Rubem Alves, "Christian Realism: Ideology of the Establishment," *Christianity and Crisis* 33:15 (1973): 175, responds that the "utopianism" of liberation theology is not a belief that a perfect society is possible, but only a belief in the "nonnecessity" of the present order.
100. McCann, *Christian Realism*, p. 203. Note, however, that most liberation theologians distinguish clearly several types of liberation—socioeconomic, liberation from sin, etc.—and therefore may indeed be able to distinguish partial from fundamental alienations and liberations.

101. Norman, *Christianity*, p. 79, goes so far as to argue that the true Christian does not aspire to a better social order, knowing full well that human aspirations are incapable of fulfillment, and remembering the injunction to "take no thought for the morrow." However, most Christian realists would not agree with this radical conclusion, though they would share Norman's conviction regarding the relativity of all human achievements.

102. Reinhold Niebuhr, letter to Hans Schonfeld, May 21, 1937; quoted by Roger L. Shinn, "Realism, Radicalism, and Eschatology in Reinhold Niebuhr: A Reassessment," in *The Legacy of Reinhold Niebuhr*, ed. Nathan A. Scott (Chicago: University of Chicago Press, 1975), p. 95. Cf. Robert McAfee Brown, "Reinhold Niebuhr: His Theology in the 1980s," *Christian Century* 103 (January 22, 1986): 67.

103. Reinhold Niebuhr, *An Interpretation of Christian Ethics* (New York; Seabury, 1979), pp. 140-141.

104. McCann, *Christian Realism*, p. 150; Weir, "The Bible and Marx," p. 348.

105. Alfredo Fierro, *The Militant Gospel: An Analysis of Contemporary Political Theologies* (London: SCM, 1977), pp. 319, 344; McCann, *Christian Realism*, pp. 204-205; Norman, *Christianity*, p. 53; Hebblethwaite, review of *Marx and the Bible*, p. 257.

106. Hebblethwaite, review of *Marx and the Bible*. In fairness to Miranda, it should probably be noted that such techniques are relatively recent and his own research may predate some new developments.

107. McCann, *Christian Realism*, p. 205. However, McCann assumes that the details of biblical narratives must "possess a high degree of historical accuracy" for Gutierrez's analogical method to apply. This is debatable. For example, though Ronald Munoz, "Two Community Experiences in the Latin American Liberation Movement," *Concilium* 6 (June, 1974): 146, argues that there is evidence to support actual parallels, he suggests that the more fertile approach is simply to understand that the same God is being revealed as liberator in history in both circumstances.

108. Dorothee Sölle, review of *Marx and the Bible*, in *Union Seminary Quarterly Review* 32 (1976): 52, raises questions about Miranda's use of Scripture. Walter Brueggemann, in *Interpretation* 29 (1975): 432, 435, calls it an "inescapable book," yet says that Miranda's methods "leave this reviewer uneasy."

109. Liberation theologian Joseph Comblin, "Freedom and Liberation as Theological Concepts," *Concilium* 6 (June 1974): 98, argues, for example, that "the biblical message of freedom is not to be found only in those texts which speak explicitly of freedom."

110. Norman, *Christianity*, p. 15. He adds that "it is the foreign clergy who are everywhere noted for their radical politics" (ibid., p. 46).

111. Fierro, *Militant Gospel*, p. 324. This criticism is directed explicitly at Gutierrez.

112. Weir, "The Bible and Marx," p. 348; McCann, *Christian Realism*, p. 187. Some liberation theologians have raised the same issue. For example Bocsak, *Farewell*, p. 12, argues strongly that liberation theology is not simply "critical reflection on praxis," but is "critical reflection on praxis *in the light of the Word of God.*"

113. Braaten, *Apostolic Imperative*, p. 100; see also Robert T. Osborn, "Some Problems of Liberation Theology: A Polanyian Perspective," *Journal of the American Academy of Religion* 51 (1983): 84.

114. Norman, *Christianity*, p. 13. Norman argues that Christianity contributes a distinctive perspective on human nature; in giving up claims to an understanding of human nature, liberation theologians give up what is distinctively Christian.
115. Braaten, *Apostolic Imperative*, p. 95: Praxis "carries a Marxist load of meaning incompatible with the gospel."
116. Fierro, *Militant Gospel*, p. 338.
117. McCann, *Christian Realism*, p. 160.
118. Some liberation theologians have noted this and moved into the "liberation of theology" (cf. Segundo, *Liberation*), or beyond Christianity altogether (cf. Mary Daly, *Gyn/Ecology: The Metaethics of Radical Feminism* [Boston: Beacon, 1978]).
119. Norman, *Christianity*, p. 75.
120. Thus, Fierro, *Militant Gospel*, pp. 330f., charges, contra Gutierrez, that the real issue is not the "nonperson" but the "nonbeliever." Liberation theology cannot assume faith, and work only at the level of dogmatic theology which works out the meaning of the faith for those who already believe. Rather, he suggests, liberation theology should be doing "foundational" theology, in which the question "Why believe?" becomes central.
121. McCann, *Christian Realism*, p. 210. Here, McCann's reading of liberation theology would appear to be accurate. Although Bonino, *Toward a Christian Political Ethic*, p. 109, offers some "theoretical ethical criteria," he also asserts that "only a living relation between the leaders and the people, only the 'sense' of what is right at any given moment, can prevail."
122. Whether revolutionary socialism will mean expropriation of corporate assets, for example, is "simply not discussed" (McCann, "Liberation," p. 52).
123. James H. Cone, "The Gospel and the Liberation of the Poor," *Christian Century* 98 (February 18, 1981): 166. Norman, *Christianity*, p. 54, charges that any new socialist alternative in Latin America is not likely, based on the experience of Chile. It should be noted that not all Latin American liberation theologians support socialism as an alternative; see, e.g., Joseph Comblin, "Freedom and Liberation as Theological Concepts," *Concilium* 6 (June 1974): 103.
124. Fierro, *Militant Gospel*, p. 361.
125. Gutierrez, *Power*, p. 100.
126. George Hunsinger, "Karl Barth and Liberation Theology," *Journal of Religion* 63 (1983): 260.
127. Weir, "The Bible and Marx," pp. 349f.; Brueggemann, *Interp.* 29 (1975): 435.
128. Emil Brunner, *Justice and the Social Order* (London: Lutterworth, 1945), p. 19.

Conclusion

1. This formal notion is widely accepted in both theological and philosophical circles. See, for example, Emil Brunner, *Justice and the Social Order* (London: Lutterworth, 1945), p. 23: "From time immemorial the principle of justice has been defined as the *suum cuique*—the rendering to each man of his due."
2. Jose Porfirio Miranda, *Marx and the Bible: A Critique of the Philosophy of Oppression* (Maryknoll, N.Y.: Orbis, 1974), p. 26.

3. Joel Feinberg, "Noncomparative Justice," in *Justice: Selected Readings,* ed. J. Feinberg and H. Gross (Belmont, Calif.: Wadsworth, 1977), p. 55. A. D. Woozley, "Injustice," in *Studies in Ethics:* American Philosophical Quarterly Monograph Series 7 (1973), also suggests that injustice is "more interesting" than justice, and has been little analyzed.

Index